THE GRL WHO BANGS

A book by Grlwithbangs
Autumn Weimann

The grl who bangs

Disclaimer

The information contained in the book and its related guides serve as a part of the author's collection of books, which may increase their income passively. The material can include content from the third party, but the author takes full charge of quoting genuine resources (may be subjected to copyright). If the content inculcated in the publication becomes obsolete due to technical reasons or whatsoever, the author or the publication house is entitled to no blames. No part of this shall be reproduced, sold, or transmitted in any medium by the third party except after the author's approval.

Table of Contents

Dedications

To all the girls who have ever cried over a boy: Pull yourself together!

To my parents, who showed me to never give up on love.

(Dad, please skip the sex scenes)

To the love of my life Joseph Weimann, let's make babies…. in 3 years.

Introduction

Looking back, there has always been one thing I wanted to do, help people. This book is simply a pursuit of it. I have always been surrounded by relationships and enjoyed analyzing them. Most of you are probably thinking, "This girl hasn't been through it all; she's young?" From what I've experienced, not just in my relationships but the ones around me, my family, and friends. I know enough. Enough to know that I'm at a place where I can share my knowledge in this world where we now consider dating with sliding into DMs & swiping right or left.

Dating, relationships, and divorces are so much more complicated today. We Millennials & now Gen Z-ers have access to so much at the tip of our fingers. It's quick, sneaky, and easy to be brave behind the keyboard. This is a book about turning your heartbreaks into happiness. Finding fun in your dating life, married life, or just be HAPPY in or out of a relationship. Life is too damn short, and to dwell on pain will only bring you down. I've been there multiple times. My sisters have been there. My own parents, who have been married for thirty years, have been there. WE have all been there.

I grew up pretty fast. I went from thinking, "all guys are dicks" to now a married woman in my twenties! I've had relationships where I was being cheated on. I had bad breakups where I felt as if my world had come to an end and lost all motivation. I've had relationships where I ended things even when he was the sweetest guy ever, as I just lost interest. I've also felt empowered. Not wanting a man or needing one. I had the most important relationship, with myself and needed to focus on ME and love myself first. I then fell in love or at least thought so. I played house at a young age with an older man. I then found the true meaning of love that everyone talked about in fairy tales and reconnected with my best friend, whom I always had a crush on, ever since we were ten.

I wanted to write this book to let you know that we all have our demons. We just don't talk about them. On social media, I've gained popularity through my love story & overcoming a bad breakup. What I don't share are the obstacles we overcame and how I eventually found happiness.

I am not a certified therapist in relationships. However, I sure do have real-life experiences that do not need a certificate or schooling to tell you that this fucker is cheating on you. Or, in other cases, how you could spice up your love life!

Lastly, I pray that no one ends up with an asshole but with someone whom they truly love and loves you back for you.

This book is for you, babe, for you to see things for what they truly are, what to do in difficult times, how to overcome certain relationship pain, and, most importantly, how to be a better version of yourself. What we should be looking for in a man, and how to get you a man you deserve. It's all here!

Single Life

The Pros and Cons of Hooking Up With Your BFF

Should you? Or should you not?

You have been friends for a while now. And, THAT thought has always crossed your mind, "Should I hook up with my BFF?" I mean, what is the worst that can happen. They're your bestie, and you know everything about each other, right? Before hopping in the bed with them, you'll need to know these major pros and cons of hooking up with your friend to help you make the right decision.

Pros

1. Comfort

You both have a level of comfort with one another. That means all you ladies can skip that awkward first date when you're too shy to eat in front of him. Phew! Being comfortable around each other establishes an emotional connection. Your body language and your confidence are much higher than dating someone you don't know at all.

2. You know all About Them

I'm talking about the history of all their dirty laundry. This is probably the best pro! You know their past relationships, the ex's, friends, what they like to do, and their daily routine. It's an advantage because you already have an idea of who this person is.

3. Minimal Awkwardness

You both, as friends, have mutual respect for one another and understand one another. You already know what you have in common and what you don't – which you can use to your advantage. The point is, you've already had those awkward moments, and since you're such good friends, you don't have to really feel weird about anything.

Cons

1. Loss of Friendship

You are worried about losing them by having an awkward hookup, or you could get attached, and they don't or vice versa. The point is, your friendship is on the line. You could end up losing your best friend. Are you ready for that? Because if things go south, that's is very likely to happen.

2. No Sexual Chemistry

You hook up, and the sexual tension just wasn't there. This means you basically won't ever talk to each other again because of how weird it was. Yikes! A botched hook up can break up the friendship, and you will most likely feel uncomfortable when you see each other. If all was right, but you two just didn't click in the bedroom, it can make every encounter cringe-worthy.

3. Awkward Social Circle

You both share the same social circle since you are already BFFs. A messy hookup could lead to drama within your circle. Friends can take sides, and this could end up ruining multiple friendships, not just yours. Not only that but if you two are having fun hooking up, your friends can still make things weird by treating you two as a couple when you're clearly NOT. Talk about annoying.

This awkward situation has happened to me personally. Yup, Me! I never thought it would. I was actually the one to gain the courage and confidence to make the first move. I am now finally in an amazing relationship with my best friend of fifteen years.

We have the same circle of friends, which makes it so easy to hang out with everyone. We have secret handshakes, do facial masks together, watch The Bachelor, laugh continuously, aware of our past relationship histories, and understand each other's needs.

You only live once, and you don't want to ever live life thinking "what if" or "He could've been the one." You will never know until you try!

Stop Dwelling in the Past

And why it's not worth it

Hey girl, are you one to dwell on your past romances and can't stop thinking about them? Unfortunately, there is a flip side to reminiscing in the past.

Other than happiness, you probably also feel a lot of pain, regret, disappointment, and even shame. Know that this is also normal. It is human to suffer as an outcome of reflecting on the past. We have all experienced this in different shapes and forms.

While some of us are successful in finding relief and peace in relinquishing the past and embracing the present, many often fail to escape from the grips of the past as the heavy impact it has had on our lives.

For some of us, the past consumes our entire conscious lives and controls what we decide to do, say, and choose to be. Perhaps most regrettably, dwelling in the past sabotages and gradually undermines our relationships with our friends, family members, and in finding a partner.

If you feel dominated and drained because of your past, let me help guide you to help find your peace.

Why Do You Live in the Past?

Why do some people fail to let go of the past, while others live more in the present moment? There could be various reasons. If you do live in the past, you most likely:

- You were raised in an environment that encouraged such habits (you might have parents who mourned over the past).

- Inherit a certain biological or genetics that predisposed you to feelings of depression or other tendencies that contribute or are associated with your past-dwelling; you feel that no matter how hard you find it, you reminisce on a past love or a lover often.

- Adopted the habit of residing in the past as a method of coping (or escape) mechanism to avoid the present, for, i.e., from taking responsibility for your happiness and life. No present love seems to have your interest in the way a past lover did.

- Adopted the habit as a result of less self-esteem and the unconscious belief that "you do not deserve to be happy," further contributing to your tendency of self-sabotaging your happiness. Settling for less; a lover or a relationship is indeed a recipe for disaster.

Dwelling over the Past Gradually Destroys Your Connections with Others

There is nothing more toxic than to have a relationship as constantly living in the past. I can give you a firsthand account of what it feels like to be with a person who constantly obsesses, ruminates, and mourns over what used to be, and it's beyond annoying!

Above all, you feel taken for granted. You feel invisible, forgotten, and ignored. As time passes, you become a simple backdrop in the life of a person constantly fixated with the past. It won't be long before a huge rift or a deep gap cuts through the middle of your relationship, which could prove hard to mend.

The many consequences of living in the past involve psychologically and emotionally blocking those you love now. It involves alienating the goodwill and intentions of others towards you. It also diminishes the very essence of what makes connections with others so much joyful and fulfilling: life.

Why? Because living in the past is essential substitutes for the liveliness of the present moment, with the death and has-been of the past. Living in the past is simply living in death. But it does not have to be that way.

How to Be Reborn into the Present.

There's a good chance you've been told the old adage: The past is non-existent, dead, gone. You cannot fix it, cannot change it, and so stop trying. However, this saying might not have done much for you and made you feel further miserable and stranded. Often it takes way more to drop an addiction than simply agreeing with a saying. Living in the past is an addiction by its very nature, so do not worry. There is more to it.

So ladies, let's get down to it- here are some ways of being reborn into the present moment.

RECOGNIZE IF YOU'RE MISERY COMFORTING OR NOT.

Why would you want to opt-out of a habit that actually benefits you? While true that most habits benefit us in a variety of ways, past-dwelling is in no way exempted from this. How could past-dwelling benefit you? Most likely, it gifts you with a sense of certainty and control. Happiness and fulfillment for many of us are scary things because they cannot be controlled or captured. We rather fear transience and instability, so dwelling in the past can be a way of gaining control over the chaos in our lives and preventing us from our vulnerabilities. For, e.g., having something taken away from us like joy. Thus we take comfort in our miseries. Indeed misery is certain, misery can be controlled, and misery is familiar. Not only that, but many people also use self-imposed misery to distract themselves from the present. From the emptiness in their lives, from their fear of living with courage, from their fear of failing, from their fear of being held responsible for the result of their existence.

Living in the past can give us the key to avoiding the self-responsibility of the present. It is the highest form of avoidance.

ASK YOURSELF: IF I LET GO OF YOUR MISERY, WHAT WOULD I LOSE? Remember: YOU WILL LOSE SOMETHING.

This question takes a lot of honesty while self-inquiry. As we know, it is common for us to gain something from dwelling in the past, something of power. Whether you live in the past to avoid responsibilities of the present; to feel the control of your life; to feel like a righteous victim, or to even preserve the memory of a loved one who is no longer with you cannot let go because of the fear of living, there's something that you would lose if you would relinquish your habit right now.

But what is that something?

Once you discover with unconditional honesty what the thing is, ask yourself: So Am I ready to surrender it? Am I ready to move on to the next thing? The answer to this question will determine how much success you will have in overcoming this addiction to past-dwelling.

BECOME CONSUMED IN SOMETHING OF THE PRESENT.

The next step in the process of living in the moment is finding something to be consumed in, right here, right now at this moment. This would most likely involve fulfilling a long-held dream, like writing a book, creating a flower garden, or even cleaning out the entire house.

No matter how romantic or homely your interest might be, do it. If you do not have a long-held passion for something and/or a plan, think of something. Even the act of researching is a form of being consumed. Occupy yourself in the present moment, and you won't have time to go to the past.

Don't dwell on the past. Remember, babe, life goes on.

He can't read your mind, Ladies

This myth has been busted

So here is a secret that men want us to know: Ladies, we cannot read your minds. I can't tell you how many times my mom has said this! The inner rolling turmoil of a woman's mind frightens them. If we are not to say what's bothering us, they assume all is good. If we will not ask for help, they believe us and think we got this. They don't see the countless safety hazards around the kitchen. If you say you don't want anything for your birthday, guess what you won't get anything. If you say nothing is bothering you, guess what he will think nothing is bothering you! So why do most of us play these mind games and not just tell them what's really on our mind?

We have to ask to get help, say what we are thinking, and out loud. We have to ask for what it is we want. Because if we don't, they just won't know.

No, seriously. Our men may not be holding out on us. They are not secretly planning how to hurt you by not opening the car door like they did when you were dating. Not also to give you a complex about whether or not our relationship still has that spark when they check their phone during dinner. They simply don't know.

And so, we must ask.

I know, I know. This feels like breaking all the womanly rules you've been taught. Damn you, Cinderella. We have been hushed to keep our little dreams and desires quiet and to ourselves. Don't say it out loud, as Cinderella urged us, or it won't come true. Sorry, Cinderella. Saying it out loud is the only way to establish communication.

Men and women are wired quite differently – our brains behave differently and have emotions that drive us in different ways. Now it could be hard to comprehend this, but if you accept it, it will make your relationship a lot stronger! Hints and/or expectations don't work – men communicate directly. They say what they mean, usually in a concise way. This is how they operate; they interpret things more literally and don't read into words as we do. Their thinking is quite linear, whereas women think in a more 'mixed up' way.

Using an analogy, women's brains are like a huge plate of spaghetti. We are all over the place with our thoughts and emotions. We can have multiple things on our minds all at once. Men's brains are like a closet of boxes. They only have one box open at a time and can only give their full attention to the open box.

We also have a vast difference in our communication. For example, we've all been through the "I'm fine dilemma. Chances are with a man, if he says he's fine or that's all's okay, it probably is. But with us women, it never really quite is, is it?

So what does a Gal do?

First things first, it's not a crime to admit it when you're hurt. No need to keep that pain inside, it will just keep on pinching. Don't keep the burden of pain on your shoulders. Sharing it with your significant other helps in dropping the weight once and for all.

Are we sure your signs are obvious to others, but you? Texting him less than you normally do and cutting back on the emojis might seem like a huge deal to you, but he might not even have noticed the change. That is why you actually have to tell him that you are, in fact, pissed at him. Otherwise, he is never going to figure it out.

Little mind games are fun, but it could also be your delusion. If you want your crush to ask you out, then stop playing your mind games and tell him how you feel about him. Or maybe you want your boyfriend to pitch in more around the house, then stop passing those nasty or sarcastic comments and bluntly tell him that he needs to do his fair share. Honesty works wonders, but I'm sure you already knew that. I mean, I made almost every first move with JB and tell him how I felt. If it wasn't for me doing that, who knows where we would be at now.

If you are one of the lucky ones, your man does indeed love you. If he gives a shit about you, he would not want to hurt your feelings. He would instead want to know what he has done wrong, so he will not make the same mistake in the future. If he loves you, then the last thing he wants is for you to be mad. Your demeanor can put your man in an unease, wondering what has happened and if everything is alright. Ladies, would a little transparency really hurt?

Like I mentioned, communication. If you still feel the need to be with him years from now, then you have to get used to talking to him about everything that has been on your mind—even the rough stuff. If you are meant to be, then you'll be able to handle all of the awkward conversations and petty arguments.

Many times, you yourself don't know what's wrong, remember, he isn't a magician! The mind is a strange thing, and this happens often. *"Oh, you just never know anything, do you'?* Stop it, ladies, I mean it.

You think that he should know what he's done wrong and are now waiting patiently for it to happen. Waiting for him to figure it out is only going to make the fight last much longer. You might as well get everything off of your chest. Right? Otherwise, you're going to be pissed for much longer than you need to be and pissed much longer than him.

If you want him in your life, then act like he is a part of it by filling him in. Sometimes, your own mother and BFF would not be able to figure out how you are feeling, so you cannot blame your boyfriend for not knowing, either. You're giving him an impossible task. Yes, you are impossible.

Even if he can't figure out what is wrong, you should give him credit for realizing out that you're upset. Some men wouldn't even notice that much...

Learn to appreciate a good man, ladies.

Better be happy than right.

Every now and then, listen to your heart.

We have all been there. We have found ourselves stuck in a meaningless argument that we just didn't want to drop because we knew we were right, and we didn't want to give in to a person whom we believed to be wrong. Our stubbornness and pride kept us stuck on a treadmill, making absolutely no progress but refusing to allow the other person to have the final say. All this simply because we knew we were right and wanted someone to acknowledge it.

I accept that in my own life, I desperately need this saying, this mantra. I need it because, in my own perfect little world, I AM always right!

Right?

Wrong.

I would definitely rather be happy than right— noticing that this is one of the hardest life lessons for one to learn when it comes to your loved one. It is also one of the hardest marriage lessons that I have recently experienced.

Here's the thing: I know when I have a strong opinion on something, I can dig in my heels, stand my ground, and draw that line in the sand.

But I have finally realized that sometimes, standing that ground, on my own side of that line, can be a pretty lonely place to be.

You don't always have to be right when it comes to a relationship. People will always criticize you for your decision to choose a loved one. Accept it and move on. Your girlfriends can be pretty delusional at times, and you know that. Other than that, other outside criticism that shakes your idea of your loved one is wrong. If he gets you the tingles, if only he knows how to really make you happy, stay that way.

What I do need to do more of is listen.

1. Support.
2. Allow.
3. Understand.
4. Cooperate.
5. Agree.
6. Compromise.
7. Encourage.

There are, of course, many instances when you need to make sure that everyone has the correct information so that the best decision can be made. There are many instances that we experience every day where it really does not matter who is right and wrong. And even more, instances where there is no absolute right answer, and it is simply a matter of perception or opinion. It is in these two latter categories where you run the risk of sacrificing your happiness (and the happiness of those around you) simply for the gratification of being able to hear someone else say that you are right. Let go of your ego, especially when it comes to your loved one. Unconditional love can never be experienced when the ego is involved.

What leads us to have this desire to be validated as being right? In my opinion, it is based entirely on ego. It comes from wanting to feel intelligent, important, respected, and perhaps even admired. And maybe even from not wanting the other person to have those same feelings when we don't think they deserve them. Again, meaningless, right? But what happens when both parties of the debate reach an impasse? What happens when you get to the stage where reason, logic, and even facts are only helping to escalate the argument rather than resolve it? When you reach that point, you can easily start to cross over into anger. And once you become angry, the truth no longer matters to either of you. Being right and "winning the argument" is the only thing that counts, and neither party will be satisfied with anything less. At the end of the day, love matters. Not being right. It's indeed the most beautiful feeling in the world, way better than the feeling of "being right."

Before you get to that stage, decide to put ego aside. Realize that you are in a situation from which there will be no winner, only two losers. The best next step to take is to practice civility and just agree to disagree.

Do so in a cordial manner, with kindness and respect for the other party. That way, the argument will end peacefully, with no lingering resentment on either side. This doesn't mean that you are the bigger person. Nor does that it mean that you are allowing yourself to be pushed around. All it means is that you see that there is a better way. Not every situation should lead to one winner and one loser. By taking this step, you preserve not only your own happiness but also the happiness of all involved. And this way, this better way, allows for everyone to win in the end.

"He's not good for you," or "he is not Mr. Right" or "you deserve so much better," are phrases we will hear often. While this may or may not be true in your case, I beg you to focus on what makes you happy. If you love a partner dearly, and someone who you feel true joy with, do not make what you may think is the wise decision. Listen to your heart.

Once in a while, let him be right too. Arguments are essential and unavoidable in a relationship. Let him loose sometimes. There is no harm. Be happy. That's all that matters.

A Misconceptional Partner

The enemy of love

Many of us often scrutinize everything he says and does. If it is so, your lack of trust goes beyond just a possible affair. It may be a sign that you're too wrapped up around him to take care of your mental health. Maybe he is cheating now, or he has in the past, then your concern is valid, but this is still unproductive behavior. Being obsessed with signs of cheating or even lying, whether it exists or not, is going to cause problems. It is impossible to enjoy your life when you're stuck worrying about "what your partner may or may not be doing" like a monster inside you that is slowly eating you away. You'll be harming your own mental health just because you're concerned about your relationship. If you can't trust him because he's had a history, or he exhibits other untrustworthy behavior, then you may want to end the relationship. Let me tell you that continuing in this way isn't going to help either one of you. The important thing to remember is, you will be fine no matter what happens. It may seem difficult or even impossible to believe this, but it's the truth. Your mental health comes before anything else, and your feeling that he's deceiving you will become less vivid and less important.

A delusional woman's purpose in life is to find themselves in some 'serious relationship.' Hence, they concoct these love affairs in their feeble minds, and when they don't work out (because it never started), they bash men to all hell and say there are no good ones left. Some men are definitely to blame as well because they prey on the delusional ones like those coward hunters that attack a wounded deer; she's an easy kill. Plus, dating the delusional one is that you don't have to do much because they create the whole thing in their heads for you.

The problem here is the anxiety and frustration it causes for both of the people in the relationship. You find yourself stuck in a web of negative thoughts. So you are making yourself a cup of coffee when out of nowhere, a glimpse of your man humping a certain "her" comes to mind. "Oh God, could he be" and just takes one thought really, in that direction, after which it is a downward spiral that just never seems to end.

According to Psychology Today, here are 10 psychological traits that are linked to a paranoid personality in a relationship.

- Is seemingly always distrustful or suspicious without need.
- Is highly moralistic and judgmental.
- Habitually questions the intentions of others, including spouse, intimate relations, family, or workmates.

- Is guarded, secretive, devious, scheming, or thinks others around him are that way.

- Is unbending in thoughts and ideas—stubbornly holds onto beliefs with rigid thinking.

- Holds grudges for a long time and is not forgiving of slights, even after many years.

- Is a chronic complainer and malcontent—never satisfied everything is above board or assumes something nefarious is at play.

- Claims that past failings at work, life, or in relationships have been the direct fault of others.

- Never seems to be happy—all too often is on edge, anxious, or irritated—there always seems to be a looming threat "out there."

- Strongly believes and constantly seeks evidence that others will eventually disappoint or take advantage of him.

- Often has an unrelenting one-track mind about this or that issue which you also must see as an important issue.

- Questions the loyalty and veracity of others, even loved ones, without basis or sees hidden meaning in the comments made by others.

- Since entering into a relationship with this individual, you see fewer and fewer of your old friends or family members.

- You find yourself having to account for your time when you are away from home.
- Since entering into a relationship with this individual, you are less happy, less outgoing, less social, or less confident; or you find you are more worried, nervous, anxious, or preoccupied with how he reacts to you.

Fight the battle within ladies, and get rid of such thoughts. Stop sniffing around for evidence all the damn time. I could not even begin to understand how it is for a man who has actually not cheated (yes, ladies, it is possible) and just sits around and listens to your crap. All that is said or at least thought at such time usually ends with, are you cheating on me?

He seems different, is he cheating on me?

He seems quite today, is he cheating on me?

Why has he started making his hair/ dressing up/ going to the gym, he didn't do it before, is he cheating on me?

A red spot on his shirt. IS THAT LIPSTICK! Is he cheating on me?

He seems lost in his thoughts, is he cheating on me?

Why did he answer his phone after going to another room? Is he cheating on me?

He seemed enthusiastic about Stephanie from work. Is he cheating on me?

He didn't fuck me like he normally does. Is he cheating on me?

And then we go ahead and cater to our delusions, sniffing for something, anything that could be used to help connect the dots. Sometimes even if they are not really connecting. Trying to access his phone, listen in on his conversations, trying to drop in at work, and ask him questions you have designed to help "break down the truth."

Now imagine this. If a guy hasn't cheated and is in a relationship with a girl who is delusional like this, he feels misunderstood, distrusted, the one whom he loves keeps screaming at his face. He meets a nice girl who is interested in him, but never indulges with her because he is in a relationship. Well, why not? His wife already thinks of him as a liar cheating piece of shit, right? So why not just give them the monster they think you are?

Ladies, STOP creating problems for your own damn self.

Men cheat when they're horny, women cheat when they're unhappy.

The three major reasons for cheating in women are lack of love from the primary partner, desire for sexual variety, and situational factors (like being drunk or on vacation).

As a woman, it's easy to believe the old assumptions that men are more likely to cheat, with the usual list of justifications like how they can't "keep it in their pants." Not saying that ain't true, we'll get to that later. This is becoming more and more untrue as time goes on. "Traditionally, it has been argued that women are more likely than men to cheat because they are unhappy with their existing relationships, while men are more likely than women to cheat because they may be seeking for sexual variety or a presented opportunity," says, Zhana Vrangalova, a "sexpert" at LELO and professor of human sexuality at NYU.

In some cases, the reasons women cheat are sexually motivated. To really understand these, let's dig a little deeper into why women cheat, Alicia Walker, assistant professor of sociology at Missouri State University, spent a year interviewing women who've had extra-marital affairs for her book, "The Secret Life of the Cheating Wife." She found more nuance to the fact that women cheat for sexual variety.

In her studies on women's infidelity, she found women were outsourcing the sexual pleasure in their relationships in an effort to remain in their primary partnership. "They believed that if they were to continue to go on without their sexual needs being met, they would have to break up their families as well as their partner's heart. None of the women took the decision to cheat lightly. After years and in some cases decades, of trying to improve things in their marriages, they decided to look elsewhere." In other cases, women are just unsatisfied with their relationships. This does not mean that women who cheat are always looking to save their relationship. Sometimes, it's the mere opposite: "One of the main reasons women cheat is to blow up a relationship that makes them feel "trapped" in a way," says Charlynn Ruan, a clinical psychologist. "Often, they are with a partner who seems like a nice person but is controlling, stifling, or perhaps emotionally unavailable. The woman may try to make changes, to get their partner to do couples therapy, or push their partner to meet them emotionally, but when the woman doesn't succeed in these attempts, cheating gives a reason for their partner to leave them."

With men, it's different. Study shows that the average man thinks about sex once every 5 minutes. Which is crazy! Our men, the leaders of the world, who have great responsibilities on their heads, and that's what goes on in their head. So when confronted, men minimize, rationalize, and justify their behavior saying stuff like:

Every guy wants to have sex with other women. So when the opportunity arises, he takes it.

I'm not doing anything that most of my buddies don't do. If you don't believe me, ask them.

If my wife hadn't gained so much weight—or if she was nicer to me, or more attentive—I wouldn't have even thought about going elsewhere.

Cheating? Really? I mean, who would rationally call getting a lap dance in a strip club infidelity? It's just what guys do for fun.

I'm only sexting and flirting. Where's the harm in that? I don't meet up with any of these women in person. It's just a game.

For girls, we end up cheating because our life lacks the spark we once felt. Everything is dull, repetitive, and life has just gone boring. Your partner doesn't look at you the way he once did, the sex isn't really as wild as it once was, you may or may not have tried to talk to him about it, and now just find yourself stuck in a spiral loop of a miserable process. You got out with your girls for a drink, until a certain someone shows you the attention and makes you feel young again. The way he makes eye contact with you, you know the kind that says, "I'm a gentleman, but I am also going to rip you apart" kind. One thing leads to the other, then boom! Copulation. Oh, and it will be great, trust me. But worth it? Never. No one deserves to be cheated on, even if that person is not trying hard in the relationship. Break up with them, but never ever cheat. That can really mess up a person. Don't even think that you'll get away with it, you won't. Trust me. Talk to him, tell him that you are not satisfied in the sack, so he could try harder, better. A man cannot handle the fact that he cannot satisfy his woman. He will try.

With guys, it's different, that guy that cheated on you, he might actually really love you. Probably more than anyone else in the world, maybe he didn't. It is hard for them to keep it in their pants, this does not represent their character, and it's just how men are. How do you think we got from Adam & eve to a population of 7 billion people? Men will be men. Your man thinks about other women and checks them out. Accept it. To prevent cheating, trust him, love him, and satisfy him sexually. He's got a fantasy you're not willing for? That's where it all starts. Satisfy your man. He can't cheat if there is nothing left in him to cheat. Let the sex be wild, take your time with it, and enjoy it. If he is the aggressive one in the sack, let him do his thing. If he is more submissive, bring out the handcuffs. Nothing makes a man more proud than to have a woman who's wild in the sack. At that point, even if he is being seduced, it does not appeal to him as much because he knows he has a wild animal at home, waiting for him.

A self-dependent woman

How needy am I?

A healthy relationship should leave you feeling good about yourself. You should feel motivated, loved, and full of life. But just because you want to the best version of yourself around your partner does not mean that you always will. Many times being in a relationship will make you feel self-conscious, anxious, and even needy. Being needy has both its pros and cons. Having the occasional need may perhaps remind your partner how special they are to you and make your relationship stronger. But unhealthy needs and the display of it can result in much jealousy and stress. It can also make your partner feel smothered and cause you to feel like you don't know who you are anymore. Loving and needing your partner is a wonderful part of a relationship. But an over-abundance of need can actually do more harm than good.

Signs of Neediness

Here are some signs that you are being too needy with your spouse and how to stop these toxic behaviors.

Losing a Sense of one Self.

When you are in a relationship, it is only natural that you are wanting to spend most of your time with your spouse. But there is such a thing as spending too much time together. If you spend an inordinate amount of time trying to please your spouse, spend time with them much often, or agree with them on almost everything, you will begin to lose your identity. If you would not know who you were, if you and your spouse broke up, you are likely too needy.

Over-reactions are Common.

It is normal for couples to argue every now and again, but it is not normal to have explosive arguments over nothing. Even that is common in a practical context. If your spouse is talking to someone of the opposite sex and it sends you into a flurry of accusations, it may be time to start rethinking how close you are with your spouse.

Constant Texting

Couples who are texting each other all day might seem adorable, aren't they? Yes, checking in with your partner via text is a cute and sweet way to let them know that you are thinking about them. But if your conversation seems mostly one-sided or consists of you sending more than two or three texts in a row without getting a response, you definitely have a problem on your hands.

Extreme Jealous Behavior.

There is indeed a healthy level of jealousy. We all know about it. I always say that jealousy is probably the ugliest trait someone can have. After all, jealousy is merely just the heart's way of reflecting on you that something or someone is significant to you. Feelings of jealousy should be used as a gentle reminder to cherish your partner – not as a catalyst to freak out on or control them. I was in a relationship where the man was extremely jealous, and he had no reason to be. It was a huge turn off and just showed that he needed to work on himself and not be so insecure.

Never Missing One Other.

You never really miss each other because you are aren't really apart. You have the same friends and do not spend a moment apart. This is not healthy behavior.

Healthy relationships happen when two people are still able to maintain some level of independence. Having your own hobbies and friendships that bring you joy will help you from being overly needy in your romantic relationship. Let him have his guy time even if it means x-boxing until 1 am.

Social Media Stalking is Poisonous.

Jealousy and neediness can become really unhealthy when they lead you to frequent anxiety over what your spouse is doing when you're not around. Instead of working towards developing deeper bonds of trust, a quality that is essential for a happy relationship, you use your neediness as an excuse to stalk your spouse online. You rage against or manipulate your partner into giving you the password for all of their online accounts just to settle your own worries. This is very unhealthy, toxic relationship behavior.

Desperately seeking Constant Reassurance.

"I'm so ugly," you say.

"Don't say that," your partner coos. "You're beautiful!"

Your spouse is always quick to jump to your defense or give you genuine compliments. But no matter how many times your spouse reassures you of their love for your, their attraction to your, or their loyalty to your relationship, you never believe them. This need for constant reassurance can be draining and damaging to your relationship.

Feeling Depressed When Not Together

It is normal to miss your partner if they happen to go away for the weekend without you. But falling into a deep depression or anxiety-filled panic attack at the thought of being away from your partner. Especially for an extended period of time is no at all healthy. This is most definitely a sign that you are too needy in your relationship. You need to start working on yourself and focus on your needs as an individual, not in a couple.

Work on a Healthy Communicational relationship.

Good communication is the true backbone of a great relationship. It is how couples learn to work as a team, resolve arguments in a healthy manner, and get to know one another on a much deeper level. If being needy is ruining your relationship, you need to start learning how to express yourself in other ways. Practice talking to your partner. Use "I" statements instead of "You" statements so that they do not feel like they have to be defensive when speaking to you. Explain your insecurities to your spouse so that they can have empathy for you and understand better why you are reacting to situations in a certain way.

Dating Life
Rules of the First Date

While a first date could be overwhelming, it's important to not let it

get the best of us. Otherwise, we don't get to be who we really are when

the time arrives. Here are some tips that can help you out.

Be on time.

Trust me, you really do not want to keep your date waiting. When

someone waits too long, they immediately go into "OMG. I've been stood

up" mode. Or the fact that maybe their date saw them, and left. Ouch.

That's not fun for anyone. If you are running more than ten minutes late,

be sure to text and keep them posted.

Put that Damn phone Away!

Unless you're waiting for your bestie to give birth because you know

she's in labor or there's some other dire emergency, put the phone away.

A good chance your friends know where you are, so if you don't get back

to a text, they'll understand. It's not the end of the world. You want to

make sure your date knows that they have your complete attention.

Embrace the Awkwardness.

I get it, first dates can be quite awkward. If and when you find

yourself in the middle of the silent phase, simply saying something like,

"Wow. So this is awkward. I am pretty sure there will be even more awkward silences to come," is actually the kindest honest thing to do. Address the elephant in the room, it's always a good idea. Not only that, but It also creates a sort of bond.

Honesty really is the best policy.

The first date is the best time and place to bring up what your expectations are of the future. If you have met through online dating, then take the opportunity to talk about what you are seeking online and what you hope to gain from it. If you met in person or maybe you were set up again, then get straight to the point of what you ideally want to get out of all this.

You are not a judge. Stop it!

It's important to have standards and stick to them, but it's also necessary to have an open mind. If your date comes in an outfit, you detest or have some sort of physical thing that you don't find attractive, or perhaps inappropriate, don't immediately throw in the towel. Judging is totally normal and a part of us, but judging to a point where you're not giving your date some slack or even the slightest chance, is a bad move. You can never really know who the one really is, you know.

Eye Contact, Please!

Your eyes can really let the person know you're interested or, as the case may be, bored as hell. If you know that you're one of those people who has a hard time making eye contact, tell your date. It's better for them to know it's difficult for you instead of them thinking you're just uninterested and rude.

Ask.

In asking questions, you're also creating a dialogue. When one person is just going on and on, and there's no feedback on the other end, things can go south fast. You want to pay attention to whether you're asking questions about them, and noticing if they reciprocate.

Don't Stray Too Far Outside Your Comfort Zone

If your date suggests something that doesn't sit right with you, don't do it. While they may think it's a great idea to do shots or skip out on the bill, don't succumb to anything that makes you feel uncomfortable. You are under no obligation to do something you just don't want to do, date or not.

Take a Stand If Things Get Weird

If your date crosses one of your personal boundaries or does anything else to make you realize they might just be the antichrist, don't be afraid to tell them so. You have nothing to lose because you're probably not going to date them anyway. Think of it as a favor to their future first dates.

Can we not dwell on Your Ex this time?

I mean, that's just a given. If they do ask, be as honest as you're comfortable with, but be wary of talking smack. This date is about a new beginning, and there's plenty of time to rehash your past if you get involved. If they talk about their ex, just smile and make a mental note. If they talk poorly about their ex, then ugh. They've just kissed a second date goodbye.

Don't justify your Beliefs.

If you're faced with a bit of negative judgment because of something you believe, don't feel like you need to explain yourself. Your beliefs are yours, and you're not under any obligation to justify anything. If you think Obamacare is great and they harp on you for that, don't let them feel like you're in the hot seat. We're all entitled to our opinions. End of story.

Who pays?

If they offer to pay for food and you're comfortable with it, let them. But if you do offer to pay half and they don't let you don't fight about it too much just to prove you're nice, or that "all men and women are equal" Ladies, this is not the time. Especially if it was a great night. Ending on an argument will leave a bad taste in both your mouths. Of course, if you feel like they truly aren't respecting your preference to pay, that's not cool either — and you should tell them so. Just so we are clear, I paid for Jb's, and I first date! LOL

Don't Be Scared To Cut the Night Short

It's your life, your valuable time, and you have a couch and sweatpants waiting for you at home. Don't force it if you know it's just not right for you. You don't need to grab another round or stay any longer than you want to. That's the ultimate rule you should follow — for yourself and for them. It will also keep him from wanting more and want to spend more time with you to figure you out.

Be yourself, for once, please?

Even though this is pretty basic, it is still missing somehow. Everyone is trying to be someone they think is better and fail. Too many wannabes roam around in the world today. Embrace who you are, nothings turns a man on than a woman who is no one but herself. If it doesn't, he just isn't the one.

The power of communication in a relationship

Communication is the backbone of a relationship

Fight the illusion of perfection without communication. It is an immaturity that will make true connections impossible between couples. Love is the foundation of a relationship, and communication is the pillar.

Bad communication is the root of major relationship problems. It is also one of the main reasons why some relationships end.

Misunderstanding, hatred, fighting does occur, but it can be overcome if both parties are ready to provide a total commitment to their marriage and are also ready to fight stormy periods. Also, remember talking is not communicating. Your man seems dim, disinterested. "He is cheating on me!" No, something's bothering him. Have you tried talking to him? Now, this does not mean that men don't cheat. They do all the time. But have you ever thought about the root of the dissatisfaction for him? "How dare he cheat on me, I loved him!" Yeah, well, did you tell him? Maybe you were busy telling him about how hard your day was washing dishes when he was busting his ass off to provide for the kids? After a few years, he meets a woman, dashing, who

43

feels for him, listens to him, and cares for him. She fills his head with how she is the complete opposite of his wife and acts that way too. Let me ask you, what do you think happened?

Unhappiness is directly connected to a lack of communication. Of course, we all talk to our partner, for, e.g., how was your day, what did you do. Safe to say, it is a different type of communication than how are you? Is everything okay? How do you feel about a particular aspect? Listen to them, and vice versa. But if it was this easy, why doesn't everyone do it?

One of the most common obstacles of communication is not letting your partner be who he is. I've seen so many couples, e.g., checking out a gorgeous girl passing by. The guy looks at her and goes, "wow, she is pretty," and the girl goes, "yeah, she sure is." A dashing guy passes by, and the girl goes, wow, he's cute! The guy goes, that's one handsome dude right there. But in reality, how rare is a couple like this? Why?

He chose you, and you chose him. You love each other. That does not diminish the attractiveness of others. "My man does not look at other girls," girlllll, he is a man. I hate that excuse, but hey, it's true. You look at other guys too that are attractive, do you want to sleep with them? If yes, I've got bad news, news we'll discuss later. But overall, you don't, they catch your eye because of their beauty. Stop restricting your partner from looking at other girls or guys. Better yet, stop molding your partner into someone he is not. Share your limits with each other, respect it, and act accordingly. To me, jealousy is the MOST unattractive trait someone can have. Being overly jealous or possessive behavior can be a turn-off. Expectations like these can create a secretive demeanor in your partner. Secrets mean less communication, which means more problems.

Ask questions, even the ones you think you know the answer to. Shut up, and listen to what he has to say. Talk about what you think, but do not take all of the air. Good communication and conflict resolution flow naturally when two people are open to learning about themselves and each other. Self-evaluation is important here; check with yourself, and make sure that you are open to learning. If you check-in and discover you are closed angry, blaming, and defensive or stressed, it can be hard for your partner to talk to you.

Also, having fun is important, tease your partner here and there, but do not insult them. When two people love each other, there are no longer two, but one. It sounds cheesy, but it's true. You making fun of your husband because let's say he lacks confidence, procrastinates a lot, etc. No one deserves to feel bad, and if your man makes fun of you instead of supporting you, talk to him. Doesn't work? Dump his ass. Not all dogs can learn new tricks — a huge obstacle to communication.

If you feel unsatisfied in your relationship and are lucky enough to be able to pinpoint what bothers you, tell him about it, and how important it is for you. Men and women are biologically different, and we see matters differently; hence, arguments. Try to understand his point of view and try to explain your point of view. Make things work.

But yeah, communication is sometimes always the key. Your man's ignorant? Dump him. Life's too short to be stuck with the wrong person.

Nice Guys or Bad Guys?

Who really finishes last?

"He loves me. He is nice, very nice." A little too nice, maybe?

Girls, you all know what I'm talking about. The one on the hook. Or maybe you're in a relationship with him. Doesn't matter, there's a good chance you don't feel the way you once have, or maybe you don't feel the same way about him.

It's hard, especially in a situation when you are confronted with two different personalities and find yourself fighting the inner battle. "Maximus is so loving, he takes care of me well, Takes my pictures, brushes my hair, makes me breakfast, is always there for me, drives me everywhere. Rarely do we ever disagree, his intent is to keep me safe. The sex is decent too, he has also introduced me to his parents."

"But then there's Kason. He can be such an ass sometimes! Yeah, he's handsome, but so is Maximus. Kason flirts with me 24/7. Cares about himself more than anything, and thinks of himself as the king of the world, willing to conquer it all someday. I think he will. His confidence gets in everyone's nerves, mine to at times. His attire is not the most adequate. We seem to disagree on things most of the time. Sometimes I feel he does that to piss me off. You don't really know what he is about to do next. I don't even think he feels anything for anyone but himself.

But he looks at me, that way, you know? That he might actually mean some of what he says. I wonder you know... What would it be like if I was with Kason?

Society will tell us that it is wrong and that a nice or a good guy is above all. I want to clarify by quoting the infamous Jordan Peterson, who explains what it is to be a good man.

"A harmless man is not a good man. A good man is a very, very dangerous man, who has it under voluntary control."

It's not wrong to want a bad guy. Because the bad guy isn't really bad. Yes, there is a big difference in what we think bad boy traits are vs. narcissism.

Narcissists are people who show high self-importance, superiority, entitlement, arrogance as well as the willingness to exploit others around them. They are often perceived as very attractive in initial encounters. This is usually because they put a lot of effort into their appearance and how they come across. Research has shown that female narcissists tend to wear more makeup and show more cleavage than women who score lower on narcissism. In contrast, male narcissists spend more time building up their muscle mass.

In the short term, narcissists can even seem better well-adjusted, entertaining, and generally nicer than they are. But in the long term, narcissists find it hard to maintain a favorable impression and tend to be perceived as less adjusted, less warm, more hostile, and arrogant. The evidence shows that narcissists don't appeal the long-term, committed relationships and don't do well in them anyway.

Women's mate preferences were explored by Buss and Shackelford (2008). They gave married individuals questionnaires that assessed both their own value as an individual and their preferences for a partner. Results indicated that women in the research desired men with traits in the following dimensions:

- Good Genes – Men who are masculine, physically attractive, good looking, fit, and high in sex appeal. Elements such as big shoulders, strong jawline, contribute.

- Stability – Men of high incomes, are educated and are older than the female herself.

- Good Parenting – Men who seek a home and children, who are fond of kids, who want to raise them well, and are emotionally stable and mature.

- Good Partner – Men who want to be a loving partner.

"Get a bad boy and hope your love will change his ways" is something that I have seen women often do. The way I see it, either he is a narcissist, or he's a man. A "bad boy" can absolutely be a gentleman,

49

especially to his woman. These are the traits I find, definitive of what we call a bad boy, a personality that consumes us, woman.

1. **Bad boys don't pretend**. There real. They don't care about what society may or may not think of them. They are who they are.

2. **Bad Boys Have Authentic Confidence.** Confidence in themselves, Hence their speech, their body language, all display confidence. Do not mix this up with false confidence.

3. **Bad Boys Have Attractive Body Language.** They do. They don't care. They are who they are and wear their heart on their sleeves. If sitting on a chair with your legs open is considered unprofessional, well not to a bad boy, it doesn't!

4. **Bad Boys Aren't Afraid of Rejection.** Their plenty of fish in the sea, for a bad boy. You might reject him, and so might Anita and so might Nicole, but Allison might not.

5. **Bad Boys Don't Try to "Fit In"** they don't feel the need to be what society considers appropriate. They do what they do when they want to do it.

6. **Bad Boys Don't Need approval.** They do not need validation from others. They have a strong belief in themselves.

7. **Bad Boys Aren't Victims.** They don't play the blame game. They are where they are because of themselves, and know it's up to them to deal with it all.

8. **Bad Boys Think for Themselves.** For them, they are the most important person, and hence they are selfish in a sense.

9. **Bad Boys Are Brutally Honest.** They don't really care about your feelings, especially if it tingles ignorance. They know that the truth is what will help you In the long run.

10. **Bad Boys Are Passionate.** They do what they love, or at least try, and display passion in the things that have their interest.

Is he a drama king?

Do you remember back when you first met your partner? They seemed to be so alive and fearless about passionately expressing their emotions and opinions. They were the life of whichever gathering they were part of. They seemed incredibly confident and sexy, too.

When this "amazing" person showed interest in you, you were naturally drawn and willing to step into their exciting world.

But now, their exciting world seems to be sucking you dry. You feel like you're walking on eggshells, afraid of somehow triggering another episode. You constantly find yourself so drained of emotional energy that it's hard to pursue what is important to you. You might even be avoiding being anywhere near your high-strung partner.

Making a marriage work takes a lot of effort for both parties involved... The problem is that when you're married to a drama queen (or king), it can seem like you're the only adult in the relationship because they're so busy trying to grab all the attention by throwing temper tantrums and insisting that you take **care of them regardless of** anything else is happening.

1. Recognize your drama queen's (or king's) tricks.

Here's a list of some of the common tactics used by them:

- Worships you one minute and despises you the next based on overreactions to the smallest of matters.
- Makes over-the-top showings of vulnerability in response to minor events (e.g., crying hysterically or panic attacks). More common among women.
- Avoids discussions in favor of a monologue during which they expect you to play your part (e.g., exclamations of surprise and asking "then what happened?")
- Rarely remember what you told him about what's going on in your life...
- Dominates social gatherings with stories about themselves and/or demands.
- Overshares commonly.
- Betrays secrets.
- Possible threats, including self-harm and/or divorce.
- Takes everything to heart because they're hypersensitive, highly emotional, and hurt easy.
- Misunderstands, jumps to crazy conclusions and blows up, then demands an apology from you.
- Always looking to play the blame game instead of taking responsibility for their mistakes and NEVER forgets your mistake.
- Believes that loud emotions are strong because calm people are wimps.

2. Understand the reason behind the drama.

If you're not really an emotional person, it is quite hard to really get why anyone would act like this. Because it's out of your experience.

According to Ophelia Austin-Small in her Scientific American article, there are several reasons why someone would behave like a drama queen or king:

- A personality disorder like borderline personality disorder (BPD) or histrionic personality disorder.
- Childhood trauma anywhere from abuse to natural disasters.
- Childhood neglect – physical, emotional, intellectual.
- Genetic predisposition.

3. Why are you drawn to it in the first place?

There's something about their behavior that fascinates you (or used to, at least). Maybe it's how open they are with their emotions because you might have a difficult time expressing yours. Maybe it's the limelight they often draw to themselves because you've felt like a wallflower. Maybe it's because of the feeling of importance since they need you so much.

By clearing out your part in the situation, you'll feel in power because there's something specific you can do to address your needs and start to break the melodramatic cycle of your relationship.

When your spouse starts making accusations or starts trying to steal the show, they're getting dramatic. The issue is that if they don't get the attention they're craving from you, they'll turn up the volume on their drama. And unfortunately, sometimes the drama shapes into abuse. "Abuse is a continuous pattern of behaviors to maintain power and gain control over an intimate partner. Behaviors that can physically harm, arouse fear, prevent a partner from doing what they want or force them to behave in ways they do not want to. Abuse includes physical and sexual violence, threats and intimidation, emotional abuse as well as economic deprivation.

Your life doesn't need to continuously be hijacked by your spouse's behavior and neediness. It's up to you to decide what you will and won't tolerate. For example, if your spouse demands your complete attention at any given point of time regardless of what you are doing, you can lay out strict criteria for when you will address their concerns because they are not allowed to hijack your life. Show them their place whenever required.

If you pay attention to them when they are acting out, they learn that they can get what they want by acting out and will continue to do so. So no matter what they pull – break things, insult you, make threats, throwing a fit over something insignificant, and just remain calm. Don't try to fix things for them. Also, don't insult them, threaten them, or a fit of your own. If they see they've got to you, they'll know they can get your attention by continuing to behave in that manner.

Living with a drama queen or king can be quite exhausting. You find yourself spending time taking care of you, especially after one of their outbursts. Learn what things help you to get back to yourself and out of the negativity. You might try meditation or taking a walk or getting a massage.

Putting some distance between you and your loved one when they're acting out is very important. Maybe by remembering what is at the root of their overly dramatic behavior, you'll be able to emotionally detach from an outburst. You might also remember why you are (or were) drawn to the drama in the first place and correct your contribution to the situation. However, if you've tried everything and the situation isn't improving, it might be time to consider leaving your marriage or even separating for a time.

At the end of the day, if their drama is too much for you, drop them. That is the first option, always. You do not need to give your life away to take care of someone else. You deserve a man. A Real Man!

Never settle for less

Avoid undermining your value

"We accept the love we think we deserve."

An amazing line from the movie "The Perks of Being a Wallflower" that surely struck a chord in many people.

Why? Because it's just so true.

"Settling" is another depressing word that is now popular in our millennial vocabulary, more than ever.

But it's not only a term but a common practice in modern dating. So many people settle for relationships that are not good for them because they think of the alternative that being single is much, much worse. I am guilty of this. I thought that because I lived with someone, I couldn't end our relationship and be on my own and afford my own place, so I "settled."

What does it mean to settle in a relationship? It can be difficult to determine what is settling compared to the good old compromise when it comes to dating and relationships.

But there's a huge difference. According to life coach John Kim:

"Settling does not mean to let go of preferences. We all have things we prefer but do not always get, and that is not enough to end a relationship. If someone loses their job, hair, or abs, that does not mean you are settling. Settling means letting go of things that are important to who you are, what you believe in, how you would like to be treated and loved. We settle when we start compromising ourselves and our own basic needs."

At an early age, we are programmed to tie our worth to our ability to find a partner. We are told that we are not complete until we find our other half. This has made us so desperate for validation that we often settle for toxicity. We jump from relationship to relationship, and we continue wasting our time with the wrong people because being single means we have failed. In contrast, those who refuse to settle are labeled as picky or just plain unrealistic. They are urged to lower their standards.

But why should you not fall for this stigma? Why is it so important to be with someone who knows your worth? Let's discuss this.

Do not settle for less than a person who appreciates you in every single way.

Someone who is not only holding your hand while you are walking together or is making sure you are on the safe side of the road. Find someone whose hand you can feel next to you while he walks with you through the walk of life.

Do not settle for less than a partner who does not just tell you how they feel but are always showing you through gestures that you are loved than never before.

Someone who kisses you because they cannot live without your touch. Someone who pulls you in close to them when you lie together. Someone who loves the feeling of your breath in their face while you sleep or does not mind the fact that you have made their arm dead. A person stays awake because there is something beautiful about you asleep, and he does not want to wake you.

Do not settle for less than an honest partner who brings you up to meet his friends.

Somebody who would introduce you to their loved ones with pride and would be prouder to tell them that he or she is in love with you. Someone who makes you feel appreciated and displays it to their family and friends. Stay single if you have to until you find the person who introduces you to their family as his loved one. Because that is exactly what you are. And most importantly, someone who is and would always been willing to stay by your side whether their close people like you or not.

Do not settle for less than someone who would cherish every moment you've spent with each other.

A person that is not seeing you just to have drinks or dinner at a beautiful place. Or for sharing a few moments of intimate pleasure together. Find someone who would be glad to come to see you even for a few moments and would do everything he can to be in your company. No matter where and how.

Do not settle for less than someone who treats you with utter respect and kindness.

Do not settle for less than a person who is always going to text you back. Someone who is not afraid to pick up the phone and call you even if you have had a fight. Someone who plans their future with you in it and is not intimidated by a serious relationship. Do not settle less than someone who would never take advantage of your feelings.

Do not settle for less than a person who you can fully rely on.

A person who would never play mind games or mess with your head and heart because he knows this is all childish and shows insecurity. Someone who understands what they have to offer is pure love deprived of selfishness and personal interests. A partner who is honest will always keep their word.

Do not settle for less than a partner who makes you confident and believes in you.

A person who is appreciative of both your looks and your soul. A person who makes you feel safe, desired and loved, no matter what.

Settle for someone who describes you as beautiful instead of hot. A person who is honest about the bad and good things about you. But also tells you that their judgment is out of unconditional love. Someone who understands "For better and for worse."

Do not settle for less than a partner who is fully ready to commit.

Someone who is responsible, who can maintain a serious relationship with you. Someone who has a good plan and sees a bright future both for you too. A person who is mature enough for a long-lasting and serious relationship.

Do not settle for less than a partner who realizes that hardest the part was not getting you but keeping you.

Stay with someone who realizes that after you are a couple, you need to walk a long way together. Someone who would make all they could to keep you by their side. Stay with a person who doesn't want to lose you. A person who is ready to fight for you. Someone who proves you that they are prepared to put much effort into your relationship to make it work.

Do not settle for less than a person who tries to keep the spark of love between the two of you alive.

Someone who sends shivers down your head to your toes just by touching your body. A person who makes you smile every time you see their face. Someone who is passionate about you and keeps the flame in your relationship burning.

Do not settle for less than someone who is definite of their feelings for you.

Stay with a person who says he loves you first just because he wants you to know it and would never change their mind about how they feel for you, no matter what.

Do not settle for less than the partner who makes you happier than you ever thought you could be.

The person you think of when that song comes on, and you turn the radio up a little louder. Stay single until you meet someone who, in the term, becomes your best friend.

Do not settle for less than someone who is ready to admit when they are wrong.

Someone who knows when and how to say they are sorry. A person who is not proud and stubborn. A person who would be happy to both apologize for their mistakes and accept your apologies as well. Because they know nobody is perfect.

Do not settle for less than someone who listens to you even if you keep telling them the same story over and over again.

Someone who values your opinion, even if he or she has an opposite view about the situation. Someone who wants to know how your day is going, who wants to hear what you have to say, instead of complaining that you talk too much. Instead of telling you that you are too sensitive or too dramatic, or too much.

Do not settle for less than a person who is worth the effort. Worth energy. Worth the time.

Don't waste your years on someone who only needs you when they are lonely or have no serious intentions. Don't bother with people who act like the effort you're putting in makes you desperate. Wait until you meet the right kind of partner who loves you honestly and sincerely and wants to stay in your life forever.

A healthy relationship means two healthy individuals

You need to be happy to attract happiness

Do you often feel like you need to be with someone? Is being single, a form of unhappiness to you? Or maybe it's hard for you to spend time with yourself? Do you mostly need someone to talk to, who can make you feel better about yourself or just share the burden of your Loneliness?

Girl, I've got news for you. The answer to your problems is not in finding Mr. Right. There is nothing Mr. Right can do if you are not in peace with yourself. Or better explained, if you do not love yourself.

I don't mean love yourself as in spending countless hours doing makeup, shopping, or a strict diet. Looking pretty all the time does not mean you love yourself; it just means you want to look pretty — nothing wrong with that, just a mere impact of society. You ask a guy in a relationship, how did you guys meet? "*I was out with friends, and you know me, I wasn't looking for anyone...*

But then I saw her," and that becomes a part of our narrative as women, the objective of being seen. We go out hoping a man will pick us, save us, rescue us. As Iliza Shlesinger puts it, we all go out looking for someone, we dress it up, put on the spanks, put out some meat as bait, and go: "Over here boys."

Loving yourself is the art of self-acceptance. It doesn't mean being arrogant or smug, thinking that you are better than everyone else. It means having appropriate regard for yourself, knowing that you are a worthy human being. You don't need anyone but yourself. Sure, you need a partner, but before that, you need yourself. Otherwise, not only will you continue to be unhappy, but you'll also end up making your partner's life a living hell too. We all have moments of weakness, and that's fine, but no one likes a pessimist. Insecurity is a turn-off. Do you love me? What do you love about me? How much do you love me? These questions are annoying. Imagine a guy asking you time to time; you love me, right? Do you still love me? Say it, say that you love me. UGH.

We have all seen many unsatisfactory relationships and unhappy couples.

On the other hand, we've seen decade lasting marriages too. Take care of yourself not only physically but mentally and spiritually. No person or material can bring us permanent fulfillment or joy. Be thankful for the life you have, the people around you, and appreciate even the smallest of things. Trust me, there is nothing more attractive than a self-confident, and fulfilled woman.

You cannot have a strong relationship with yourself if you are one who buys into criticism easily. Self-assessment can help us determine how much we let criticism affect us. Remember, as Aristotle would say, there is only one way to avoid criticisms, say nothing, do nothing, and be nothing. No matter who you are and what you do, you will always be criticized.

There is nothing wrong with that, don't be the one to say, "People are so rude and mean." they are. Deal with it. Do what brings you happiness, wear what you want to wear, say what you feel like. Be yourself, not a version of yourself you hope people will like more. Regardless, there is nothing more attractive than originality.

"They love each other so much..." Yup, they do. They also love themselves too, which serves as the basis of a healthy relationship. I cannot stress it enough. Are you the person that does not go out alone? Because it feels weird, awkward, or maybe you get bored. Don't be that person. Take yourself out, do things that make you happy. Stop looking for your happiness in someone else. You will be more likely to have a healthier lasting relationship without any serious consequences.

Another trait of unhappiness is selfishness. It is important to understand that the world does not revolve around us. You are not a hero, and this is not a movie. Selfishness not only molds you into an attention-seeking individual, what happens when you don't get it? Hello, darkness, my old friend. Doesn't matter how attractive you are, guys would want to do you anyways, but behind your back? "Bro, she a bitch." There is no love here. Why does this always happen to me? Because you're selfish. Plain and simple.

Also, stop being judgmental. "But I'm a woman!" I know, Stop it. We are all ignorant to an extent; some are more than others. And... judging others not only says a lot about us, most of the time, but we also end up getting false perceptions of others. Not only that, but our habits are also reflected back to us. Remember, no one likes a know it all. (Squeaky Female voice) "You know what your problem is?" No. I do not know what my problem is, and I'm sure you don't too.

Remember, the answer lies not in a man, but within. Two People happy with themselves, their life, just overall satisfied people, bring more happiness into their life when they meet another like themselves. For a relationship to work, not one, but both of you have to be self-sufficient. Many of us look for a confident, optimistic man. Nothing wrong with that, but let me ask you, are you a confident, optimistic woman?

3 Reasons He Hasn't Proposed Yet

So you're sure you've found "the one"? But, have you, really?

While there are countless reasons why your partner hasn't popped the question, these are the top three reasons why he ONLY wants to be your boyfriend, but uh-huh ladies, let's fix that!

Maybe you've been dating for a year, maybe two. Or maybe you're like some of my friends who've been doing this for TEN freaking years! It crosses almost every girl's mind at some point in her life, "so when is he going to propose?" I mean c'mon, we all have that one imaginary "wedding" Pinterest board, don't lie, especially not to yourself, at least. I even saved my contact info under "Wifey" on JB's phone when we first started dating.

After a while in a relationship, many of us assume we have to get married to this person. This is the so-called next step. Everyone else is getting engaged from high school days, so why hasn't he proposed yet? Should I ask him? How do I bring it up? This was exactly my school of thought when I was with my ex. I thought I had a timeline and which I had no progress on because I compared myself to the relationships of others. Thank goodness my ex, he always ignored the question when asked what the next step in our relationship was. I could've taken it too far, and for the wrong reasons.

Don't get me wrong, not all of us obsess over getting married and are familiar with such frustrations. Some women are more patient than others. While others need constant validation, some need little, and some need none.

Definitely, social media does have a huge role here, especially when your news feed is constantly piled up with wedding proposals, preparations, and all that. The world isn't' as real as it used to be before. "She had the best proposal on Instagram! I want one too, or "Sighs. I wish I could have something like that" all of it could easily bring you down, but it shouldn't. Everything is so over the top these days, and I strongly believe to not let it validate your happiness. Don't rely on a wedding or proposal to determine your happiness.

With that being said, here are my top three reasons why he hasn't proposed.

1.   He wants to be "financially" stable

Have you ever heard a man say, "I just want to be financially stable first so that I can take care of you?" Ladies, take care of your own damn self. I was always taught to make sure to build my own financial stability without a man. I do, however, agree and disagree with him, waiting to

THE GRL WHO BANGS

be financially stable. If you know he/she is the "The One" then why wait? Life is too short, and one could never know what could happen next.

On the other hand, it's great that he wants to have his career figured out and be financially stable. He will have a clearer head and be able to commit, especially after financial stability. For a lot of men, their egos are fed when they get to take care of their women. I think it is a great idea to wait and let him reach his ultimate goal of his dreams, his career, and having that savings account. There has been a lot of pressure in society for the man to be the breadwinner. It has reduced now but still exists. Or he's simply saving for a ring. He wants to make sure you "get the ring you deserve," right?

2. He's comfortable

A lot of men get very comfortable in their relationship, and they're scared of changing anything about it. Why change things when everything is great? I mean none of his "bro's" are married, nor engaged, so the need to rush does not really exist. Or maybe he's thinking that life is good right now and that getting engaged will just complicate things. And then, of course, marriage means less sex; and before you know it, the sexiness is gone. This perception, even though it exists commonly, is false. It's up to the people in the relationship to make it work in whatever way they want.

3. Your man is an over-thinker & just doesn't know how?

He could have previous bad experiences. Maybe he has trust issues in relationships, or he grew up around bad marriages. He has a fear of commitment because the term "a lifetime" scares him. He hasn't really put in much thought in it, or how to do it. He doesn't want to settle down because he thinks he will lose his "freedom" of guy time and would have to worry about kids, and so on.

So ladies, breathe. I have one huge take away from my personal experiences. Stop focusing on the idea of getting married as something that needs to happen as soon as possible, just because you think the time is right. Both of your opinions are valid and need to be communicated to each other. Put energy on time you spend together and strive to strengthen your relationship. I promise this will raise your chances of him getting down on one knee and saying those four special words.

Why he threatens to leave

And what to do? Help him pack his bags.

Is your relationship a tumultuous one?

A relationship where small disagreements or saying the wrong thing often leads to big, dramatic confrontations which usually result in you or your partner slamming doors, throwing stuff around, or threatens to leave? Maybe your relationship with your boyfriend has become a roller coaster of emotions. Or your decades-long marriage has been a rocky road for quite a while. And you find yourself walking on eggshells each day. You have to watch what you say to your partner and how you say it because they often take things the wrong way. You do not like to ask for anything or disagree with them for fear of creating an argument. So, you shut down and instead say, "Whatever you want, hon."

Maybe they have a controlling behavior. They get irritated with you when you do not respond to their text right away. They question the things you buy for your own self and whether they are necessary. They change the channel if they do not like the program you have selected, without checking with you first. Or they are jealous and suspicious. They interrogate you about where you have been and who you were with. They think you are cheating on them when all you are doing is work overtime or being friendly to a neighbor. Or they have a hair-trigger temper.

They embarrass you by saying mean things in front of friends and family. They bicker with you in public, because they did not like what you had said, or how you said it, or a certain on your face when someone made a comment.

You try to talk it through, reassure your partner, make amends, and sometimes placate them. But if it is not one thing, it is another.

You Love Your Partner, But you just ain't sure if you can live with them anymore. Granted, when things are going well, your relationship is passionate, intense, and deeply gratifying. Your sex life may even be more incredible. But on a bad day, which may be more often than not, you feel so alone and unhappy. You do not know what to do to make your partner understand your point of view. You do not know how to make them understand that you love them and are committed to the marriage. Happy couple smiling, nose to nose.

On those frequent bad days, you may have a lot of negative thoughts about your partner. You run a tally of all their faults. You fantasize about what it would be like to be single again. But you cannot leave or do not want to, so you feel stuck. If this describes your life, you are not alone. Many couples suffer in this type of high-stakes relationship where one person overreacts to things or often threatens to leave as a way to gain and maintain control of their partner.

But there is something important I need you to know about your relationship, which is this: it is not hopeless, there are things you can do today to bring more calm and stability to your love. It just takes understanding what your REAL PROBLEM actually is, and what to do about it.

Is Your Problem Your Partner's envy, controlling demeanor? Or something else? You might think: Things would not be so bad if your partner was not so jealous, overly sensitive, or controlling. You have tried handling these issues the best way you could to fix the problem and make your life easier. You always tell your partner, "I love you" all the time. You take care to phrase your displeasure in a way you think will avoid a fight. You make sure to call them and let them know you are on your way home from work, or if you are working late. You do not spend money unless you discuss it with them before. You often compliment them about how attractive and sexy they are. You make sure to stay close by their side when you are out in the public, touch, and kiss them often.

But no matter what you have done to keep things on an even and avoid the fights and accusations, nothing seems to help for long.

It is as if your partner forgets of all the good things about your relationship and holds on to the one thing that you said or did that proves that you do not love them, you do not care, or that you are a terrible mate. You keep repeating the same type of arguments, and nothing is ever resolved for long. And the reason that happens is due to the fact that what you THINK is the problem is not really the problem. The real problem is not that your partner is jealous or that you do not know how to be loving enough to them. Those are simply symptoms of a much bigger underlying issue in your relationship. In other words, there is a major flaw in the way your relationship is operating.

And once you understand this bigger issue and what to do about it, it's SO MUCH EASIER to resolve. You don't need to walk on eggshells, you don't need to stuff down your feelings to keep the peace, and you don't have to feel so alone anymore. Unless you have the tools, you need to fix that underlying flaw, those damaging symptoms...The rage and fighting and jealousy?

They'll keep showing up. Your partner will continue to accuse you of being unloving and uncaring. Or of betraying their trust when you've done no such thing. No matter how thoughtful, attentive, or transparent, you try to be. And the drama will continue, until one day, when your partner threatens to leave, they actually will. Because no relationship can survive that much turmoil and anxiety for long. The Mudslide of Insults, Drama, and Threats That Destroy Relationships

Divorces or break-ups never happen like an earthquake—without warning, the earth one day just opens up and cracks your relationship apart.

It's more like a mudslide. Millions of tiny raindrops pound and saturate the soil, loosen the foundation, and the weight of it just pulls the earth down and ultimately destroys it. Relationships die in small acts of destruction. They die when small disagreements frequently lead to hurtful, verbal outbursts. They die when you do everything you can to make your partner feel loved, and they accuse you of being unloving. They die when one partner constantly threatens to leave, and the other partner gets sick and tired of walking on eggshells. They die when you keep trying to "fix" the symptoms and ignore the cause of your fighting and drama.

That's why it's important that you learn what the deeper, underlying issue is in your relationship, and do what it takes to resolve it for good, so your partnership becomes strong, stable, and secure. Do not, under any circumstance, forget your value. Your partner may, and threaten to leave. Let him go. No relationship is worthwhile if your partner is threatening to leave. It's a two Way Street if he wants out to pack his bags.

Love can fog reality, we bare disgrace of our loved ones primarily because we know that they love us deep inside. But the reality is one who loves you would never threaten to leave you based on an agreement. Plus, if he is saying this now, what about later? Pack his bags and say your goodbyes. Many play this game to manipulate their loved ones. For them to be more submissive and assist them. Do not become reliant on a person so much that you let them manipulate you. You do not need anyone. Certainly not someone who does not value your love.

Unconventional Dates for the Unconventional Couple

By: Cambria Rodriguez, my sister

Are your dates boring, basic, and redundant? Is your relationship stuck in a rut? "Dinner and a movie" is so 1940. It's time to make your dating life exciting and adventurous.

In the past ten years of my life, I have pretty much always been in a relationship. Every weekend for literally a decade, I was always asked, "what do you want to do tonight?" and the answer leads to some cliché, lame couples outing. When I was FINALLY single and hit the dating world, it was scary, and I was definitely out of practice. In efforts to make myself more comfortable and the excitement to meet new people, I decided to plan the most spontaneous and creative kind of dates. From going to strip clubs on first dates, going to the ice rink just to watch people fall, playing hide-and-seek in creepy parks, to flashing taxi cabs during a city-scavenger hunt, my dating style is unconventional, to say the least. Despite this, my dating adventures have always had a 100% success rate for both involved. Doing something out of your comfort zone allows you to not only avoid the initial awkward phases of dating but open up. It helps you become more comfortable emotionally and......

what I know you really want....PHYSICALLY.

For the spooky girl looking for some thrill:

Disclaimer: this date can potentially be illegal, depending on where you live. If you want to avoid a trespassing fine, pass this section. Still interested? You're a perfect fit then! My first recommendation for a fun, flirty date is a dark park game of hide-and-seek. Yes, you're probably a grown adult, but everyone loves an excuse to be a kid again. Find a decent-size park (or even a graveyard if you REALLY want to get freaky) with lots of great hiding spots. Pack a picnic and some wine and watch the sunset. When the sun sets, let the games begin! Not only will you get some exercise in by running around the park, but the thrill of the game will boost you and your date's adrenaline. This can play in your favor during sexy time later (wink, wink).

For the city girl:

When I moved to London, I found that living in a city can be quite redundant when it comes to dating options. In London, I found that there are only two options for a night out--go to a pub or a club. You may think there are lots of options for you if in a big city, but how many times will you go to that bar, coffee shop, or art show until it gets boring? Spice it up by setting up a city scavenger hunt. Have you and your date write down at least four things you want the other person to do/find. This can be a huge personality test for you and your date too. It can show how you/them handle embarrassment, and how ballsy and outgoing you/them can be. My date made me hit up a dance floor, vigorously rock an air guitar, and then ask someone to hold my imaginary guitar for me. The poor stranger was so confused when I asked him to hold my air guitar. Among other embarrassing things, I made my date look for a black cab and flash his ass at it. This type of date is a great way to explore your city uniquely while discovering more about your date's personality.

For the confident girl:

This last option is definitely not for every girl, but it is my top recommendation for an unconventional date. If you're an over-protective girl and/or need constant attention from your man, this option is NOT for you. Additionally, I highly suggest you feel like you know your date well enough to even propose this as an option. I have done this twice FOR A FIRST DATE, and in both experiences, it was an incredible success. I met a guy for a first date at a bowling alley (eww, basic), and I jokingly suggested after a few beers that we should go to a strip club to spice things up. Of course, he was completely down for it. In another first date, we awkwardly started at a bar, quickly started hitting it off, and got caught up in beers and tequila shots. The liquid in me gave me the courage, I suggested, yet again, we go to a strip club. He was completely shocked and didn't take the suggestion seriously. But to his surprise, we ended up at a strip club on a first date, AND he got so into it that he got us a private room. Not only will the guys be bragging about this date for years to come, but it shows how cool and confident you are in yourself and your sexuality. With my great experience, I have inspired friends to do the same with their s/o. They've all had raving reviews about how this has not only been a pleasurable break from the conventional dating life but improved their sexy time in the bedroom.

Some tips if you've never been to a strip club: first, go with friends to get to know the ropes before you take a date. There's specific unspoken strip-club etiquette you have to abide by. You must purchase at least one drink, and you NEED to tip the dancers when they approach you, especially if you're a female. Other than that, be respectful, cheer those dancers on, and have a great time!

Meeting new people shouldn't be scary or uncomfortable for you or your date. It should be a fun experience where you can learn more about yourself and the boy/girl you've been crushing on. Get out of your comfort zone and plan something creative that you can talk about for years to come. Make it memorable and unique, and I promise they'll be coming back for more.

Break-up Articles
Breaking Up With Someone

5 Things that'll Take Your Mind off it

After getting dumped on Valentine's Day (twice), getting cheated on, and finding disgusting text messages on his phone from other girls, THIS one's probably a favorite and easy.

Breaking up with someone isn't an easy thing to do. Even if they've done you wrong, it's hard. Here's what you need to do right after a breakup.

You thought he was the one, you spent every day with him, you even ditched your "girl time" to be with him, and now it's all over. You feel like your world is ending, and you've lost everything. Worst of all, you're probably feeling quite insecure.

Well, it's now time to wipe those tears away and read about the five things you need to do to get back up on your feet after breaking up with someone.

1. Break up Party

A breakup party was the best idea I've ever had. Invite all your friends (old and new) and definitely invite that cute boy you've always

THE GRL WHO BANGS

had a thing for. The day I broke up with someone was the same night I had the party. I cried, had drinks, laughed, and finally kissed my childhood crush, all in the same night. Yes, I was only single for four hours. But who is to say, moving on too fast is "too fast?" After breaking up with someone, throwing a party is totally worth it. You'll rekindle with your friends and get your mind off of what happened.

2. Delete Everything

Let's start with his phone number. Okay, so what if you have it memorized? Still, delete it! Even though you look super cute in that picture with your ex, delete it! Delete every memory you have with him on social media. This gives you, your phone, and your social media a clean slate. You don't have to be reminded of his face again. And don't even think about backing up those photos to a flash drive! After breaking up with someone, you need to clear your mind and not be distracted. Deleting them from your life is the best way to do that.

3. Throw Everything Away

This might be the hardest thing to do, but you can do it! Get rid of everything. You want a fresh start and a positive atmosphere around you. Yes, ladies, even that cute necklace he got you, toss it out. Better yet, burn it all! I had a fire pit in my backyard, and it enjoyed burning my memories. This is especially true if you're the type of person who tends to use those items as a way to justify getting back with that person.

Don't! Get rid of it all as soon as you can, and your future self will thank you.

4. Make New Goals

Now, this is the time to focus on yourself and your needs as a single person. I wrote down all my goals for the rest of the year. I wanted to travel and blog more. I went to the gym almost every day. Going to the gym was probably one of my favorite goals that I accomplished. I wanted to get fit, but more importantly, I did so for myself, my health, and to get my mind off things. Focusing on yourself after breaking up with someone is the best thing to do. Work on yourself, and you'll feel amazing.

5. Stay Busy

Keeping yourself busy is key. Maybe you're not used to being alone, and when you are alone, your mind wanders, or even worst, worries. Go out with your friends or learn a new craft. Coffee shops are my go-to place. I would go to local coffee shops and blast music in my headphones.

Just remember, everything happens for a reason. I hate to sound cliché and use that phrase, but it is so damn true! The breakup just indicates that there is someone else better out there for you. Focus on improving yourself, and the right person will come along.

I'm not ready for a relationship right now."

What do they mean?

"Milo loves me.... I know it in my heart he does... he just can't commit to me right now because....... Bullshit!"

"I'm not ready for a relationship," ladies, the "with you," is silent.

Call bullshit when you see it. It's hard when we are the one on the hook, and our emotions can fog the reality of the matter. "Oh, he wasn't really the relationship type, you know," No girl, he just did not love you. You had a nice ass, hey wanted a piece of it, and that is all.

But that's not the only reason. Let's talk about the most common reasons as to why he won't commit.

Past relationships that sucked. We're all made from our experiences. Everything, even our thought process, automates from what information is given to him. We all have a perspective of guys, relationships, dating marriage that we learned from our experiences. Some have it hard and have never really been a part of a healthy relationship before, so for them, it's like a downwards spiral, nothing much to come out of it.

He just isn't over his ex. *"I sometimes see him in the middle of the night, lying down next to me, lost in his thoughts. Does he still think* *about her?"* Okay, that's a little exaggerated. But maybe there was a girl that he gives his heart out to, and she stepped on it. That pain needs to be dealt with. With a lot of guys, the "macho man" in them does let them moan about a certain pain, so they block it completely as if it never happened. That shit is unhealthy in the long run.

He's thinking of another. Maybe a certain girl at work just keeps teasing him.

Flirty girl at work sees your man

"Oh shit, hold me for a second"

"Why what happened, you okay?"

"It's just that black t-shirt you're wearing gets me wet every time. Wink"

Guy walks away, blushing

It could be confusing when you're in a relationship, and someone flirts with you. If they're okay, you'd maybe handle it. But what if their extremely hot and know how to play the game, they will not give up until you give them what they want. That's when the real battle starts. *"My girls the best, but damn, that ass... OMG"*

Where's he at? Maybe he was into dating because he wanted to have a good time. Which generally means sex. The goals weren't really to find a partner.

Money! Many guys do not commit to a girl because they have built a mountain of wealth and just don't love you enough to bring her along for the ride. Sad but true, and that just means he doesn't know what love is all about.

Romance Junkie. Many men are truly addicted to the idea of falling in love. They truly believe that. These men love to flirt; they enjoy getting to know new women. It's not really a game for them. Think of it more like a hobby.

Pressure Cooker. Even in a loving relationship, some men will feel they are being pressured to take it to the next level when they aren't quite ready. Give him a little time to figure it out, but if you sense that you are pressuring him, ask him how he feels and don't let him break.

Responsibility. Sure, he may like spending time with you, that doesn't mean he is ready to hold the throw-up bucket for you. If you are moving towards your late 30's and your baby clock is ticking, He might feel he's too young or just not ready to handle the alarm going off.

Sex! A tough pill to swallow. He wants you, or let's say, some sections of you. A Guy might know deep down that you aren't the one, but they will stir you along because they like you on their arm. Perhaps they just like your company. This is where you need to take the steering. Make him decide, It is your right to know whether he is serious or not.

It's you. He likes you but doesn't love you. It's too late, and you cannot force someone into loving you.

While sometimes you need to move on, there are situations where you need to stick with him. Maybe he did have bad past relationship experiences, does that make him a bad person? No. It's different if you don't want to put in the extra effort and drop him instead, but know that he will love you when you make him see that you are, in fact, the one.

Try to put yourself in his shoes. In a relationship that is going well, it can be hard for you to understand that maybe your boyfriend isn't ready to fully commit. That doesn't necessarily mean that he doesn't love you or wants to break up; it just means that he needs more time to adjust to the idea of "settling down."

Also, remember to give him some space for once! This doesn't necessarily mean you need to completely remove yourself from his life or break up. Just because he can't commit now doesn't mean he won't commit later. Allow yourself to give him a little distance; start hanging out with your girlfriends more or pick up a new Pilates class at the gym.

It's important also to not overthink the matter. By giving him some space to figure out his feelings, you may find yourself trying to develop the probable cause of his sudden fear of commitment. Try to restrain from over-analyzing the situation.

Also, don't fall into the trap of ultimatums. It is a tricky situation because you never want to wait around for somebody. Be that as it may, making your boyfriend decide between committing and breaking up could end up with you getting your feelings hurt.

Motivation to Get You Back on Your Feet After a Bad Breakup

It's hard, but it's doable

Going through a bad breakup is never easy. I've definitely had my fair share of breakups. Losing someone can make you feel all kinds of negative emotions. You can't get out of bed; you can't eat, you don't know or don't want to know life without your partner. Girl, you got it bad! Here are some tips to get you back on track.

First and foremost, stop stalking your ex. DELETE the EX from every social media outlet possible. Better yet, block them! The only way to move forward is by forgiving your ex. No matter what. I've always had a tough time forgiving an ex. Trust me; it is so much easier to move on once you forgive.

You probably went out a lot with your ex, or you spent money on him/her. Were you the sugar momma? Now is the time to spoil yourself! One of the first things I did after a breakup was getting a massage & facial. With makeovers, you feel like a new woman, ready to take on the world. Your confidence level is back up, and you feel fresh! I have a habit of giving myself a makeover with a hair change. I dated one guy that hated whenever I dyed my hair black. He said I looked like a porn star.

Rude, I know! So right after we broke up, I dyed my hair dark back again. I loved it!

Spoil yourself with a gym pass! The gym was my go-to place to get my mind off of things. It's a kind of therapy; the only difference is the hot, sweaty guys walking around. Not only that, but there's also nothing better than a sexy revenge body. Also, eating healthier. Okay, so you had a couple of pints of ice cream, an extra-large pizza, and maybe some wine too. It's okay to splurge that first night. However, eating healthier doesn't only make you feel better but look better too.

Take that cooking class you always wanted to do. Get back into your hobbies, or find a new hobby. My hobby was blogging. It kept me busy as I would do photo shoots constantly, which boosted my confidence levels. Plus, your mind is surrounded by positive vibes and occupied with creativity.

This is your time to figure out your purpose in life. We become so much stronger when we get rid of the extra weight that had kept us down. Going through breakups can make us not only stronger but smarter and healthier. So go get that gym pass and start working on becoming a better version of your current self!

Verbal abuse survivor tactics

By: Sabrina Rodriguez, my sister, and a survivor

The feeling of anxiety, loneliness, nausea, and depression caused by verbal abuse. This will all go away, ladies and gentlemen with NO RESPONSE. This vicious circle will keep going on forever.

Surviving verbal abuse is no joke. Sometimes it's worse than physical abuse. Those disgusting texts, voicemails, and words you hear and see can affect you for the rest of your life. DON'T LET IT. This is how I survived a hurricane of emotions and feelings through a verbally abusive relationship.

First things first, don't respond to any nasty name-calling, body degrading, and threatening words. The cycle will continue. The suppressor likes to upset you and hurt you, as they don't care as much. The best thing to do here is no response. They hate it. In fact, block their phone number or social media accounts if they go on a rampage.

You're going to need a lot of love and comfort from friends and family. I was so scared to tell or show my friends and family how I was being behaved to. They did, however, made me realize that I didn't deserve it and that no one does. Spend time with friends and family and people who bring you up and are positive influences. Talking to a therapist is also a very good idea. Sometimes there are things we like to keep private from our family and friends. There is a lot of help offered by our communities and churches for support and groups for advice.

Start over and dump all the old stuff into the trash. I moved out of my toxic relationship and got storage for all my stuff. One day I decided to throw all the old memories away. For example, blankets, kitchens necessities, and other miscellaneous things that made me think of the abuser. It's hard to get rid of anything that reminded me of the abuser, but I tried my best to turn the page and start a new chapter.

Go out and get a makeover! Financially, I know some people struggle, and so do I. I highlighted my hair. I even got my teeth whitened, started painting my nails, and bought some branded makeup from Ulta that I never had. Workout at the park or with some friends at a gym will boost your self-esteem. I lost a lot of weight from stress and depression. Working out helped me mentally, kept my mind positive, and I started to even gain muscles, and feel good about myself. Working out isn't just about losing weight; it's good for your health and soul too. I started physically taking care of myself and began to feel better, both mentally and physically. Once I put my mind to it, I realized anyone could do it.

Grab some friends and go out. This doesn't have to be all the time. It's important to realize to take time for yourself. That doesn't mean going to work or spending time with your kids, rather do something you like to do. You can go to the movies, shopping, dancing, coffee dates and or read a book. You will be surprised how much this will help make you feel.

Respect and honor yourselves, ladies and gentlemen. Don't let someone tear you down or try to ruin your life. Life is far too precious and short. Let's lift one another up and be positive influences. Support each other, and don't be afraid if you're a victim of abuse.

Marriage
Body Language Hacks

Body language, it turns out, makes up the bulk of how we communicate. While it's debated among experts, many believe this is the breakdown of how we communicate:

- Body language: 55%
- The tone of voice: 38%
- Words are spoken: 7%

Verbal communication is obviously important, but the real answer lies in your body language. Do it right, and it can really get a man going. So let's talk about it, shall we?

Don't sleep on the power of a smile!

We all know that the smile is powerful. But how you smile matters. Make sure you're giving him a smile that engages both the lips as well as your facial muscles, which is genuine and involves the eyes, rather than a Pan Am smile, which is the false smile we often see on flight attendants who are less than thrilled to bring us another pillow on a flight. When your smile is real, he knows that you're happy being with him. But not just that, he'll feel good talking to you, wanting more. Isn't that what we all want?

THE GRL WHO BANGS

Give him a sexy smile that says, "I'm thinking about what being in bed with you would be like." Not a smile that says, "Come to me, my precious."

Touch him... Subtly.

Kristine: constantly rubs Brad's chest, running her red fingernails up and down his biceps.

Lauren touches his arm once or twice on a date. Brushes her knee against his "accidentally" under the table.

While Kristine is sending signals that in no uncertain terms she wants to ravage Brad, Lauren takes a more subtle approach. She wants him just as much, but she has the decorum to communicate this tastefully. More importantly, she makes him wonder.

Avoid Crossing of Arms:

A no brainer. This is one of those signals you want to avoid because crossing your arms can indicate that you're not interested or that you're disconnected from the situation. It can also say that you're feeling insecure. If you find yourself crossing your arms (even if you're not feeling any of the things I said it communicates), simply uncross them and lean in toward the man you're with.

Power Poses.

Amy Cuddy conducted a study where subjects took either high-power or low-power poses. Those in high-power poses (think: hands-on-hips like Wonder Woman) felt more confident and performed better in tasks. You can apply this to your own strategy on how to seduce men with body language; standing with your legs spread, your shoulders back, and your hands on your hips will make you feel like a million bucks, and that will be communicated to him!

Maximize lip time!

Another versatile tool when it comes to how to seduce men with body language is your lips. There are so many things you can do with them! Start with the color. Bold colors tend to get more attention, and red is known to communicate passion. But if you're not comfortable rocking the red, try a deep berry. Really, you should just be comfortable with whatever color you choose. Licking, biting the lips, really does turn a man on! Sometimes the old school stuff does wonders for a promising relationship. Its 1980s adult film stuff, ladies, I know. But if you want his attention and have not had much luck so far, anything to do with your lips can win you the game.

Applying even a liner or gloss in front of him can drive his attention faster than you might think. Men obviously love women's mouths and why not –they are lovely things and allow us to express ourselves in a variety of ways. The mouth is key to self-expression. Make sure that you don't go overboard, being too predictable with the lip game. There should be an element of surprise.

Hair Play.

Your hair is another great seduction asset; there are a million ways to play with it to get a man's attention. Pull it all over one shoulder, toss it back, twirl a curl around your finger, and put it up in front of him. Just don't overdo it with the hair! Pick one or two tactics, but don't go overboard.

Facial Expressions.

Did you know we make about 25,000 facial expressions a day? Our faces are much more expressive and communicative than our voices ever could be. So use your face to tell him what's on your mind. Start by simply showing that you're paying attention to what he's saying. Nod occasionally while he talks. Tilt your head to one side. This reveals your most vulnerable spot: your neck. It communicates that you trust him (even if he's a vampire!). You can also mirror his expressions. If he smiles, smile back. If he furrows his brow, do the same.

Lean In.

When you lean in toward a man, he feels like you're engaged and interested in him. If you lean away, it shows disinterest. So when he's talking, lean forward just a few inches. It's a subconscious signal that will make him all the more attracted to you.

Neck Extension.

In the animal kingdom, females often showcase their necks as a mating sign. Considering we are, also animals, this is a unique way to appeal to his animalistic-side, if that's what you want (wink). We do similar dances to animals when mating. While some of our dances have changed for the better or worse, the point is that it is part of our DNA, and somewhere in our genes, we still understand this non-verbal language.

Fingers.

Use your fingers to brush any certain part of his body. You can run your finger on his arm, up to his back, along his jawline, down his nose, or across his lips too. Let your fingers do the talking. When you touch certain parts of his body with fingers, you are saying that you want to touch him more. As we've learned, men love the language of touch. Thus this will be speaking to him directly. The more you use touch, the more he's likely to pay attention to you, and the more likely you are to be on his mind later on in the day.

Whisper.

Get close to his ear and whisper. Say anything, I mean anything. He will go crazy. The closeness of your lips to his face, the heat of your mouth, your breath on his neck, and in his ear, and the sounds of your tongue moving in your mouth will drive him nuts. If you are looking to ignite his engine and make him fall for you, then start by whispering

little nothings in his ear. It really can be nothing.

Everyday Romantic Gestures to Keep the Love Alive

Romantic gestures are like the cherry on the top

When JB and I worked on different schedules, we needed to figure out how to keep the spark alive. Yes, we live together but often end up not see each other for two days! However, I always remind him that he's on my mind. I barely have time to do my hair for work, so how can I make time for romantic gestures every day? Sometimes the most meaningful gestures can be found in the smallest of things. So how do we keep our fire blazing?

I usually wake up early for work. I wake him up with tons of kisses all over his face and say, "good morning!" He usually goes back to sleep after, but waking your partner up with kisses is the best way to wake up! OR, if you are really in the mood- there are other (sexual) things to do to wake your partner up. I love to write love notes around the house. I usually leave notes by the coffee pot, so he sees it in the morning. Making love notes funny or corny is so FUN! Don't live together? Leave cute notes in their car or butt pant pockets.

While we are both at work, I like to send quick and random text messages like "I love you, can't wait to come home." It's so easy to text someone these days, and it literally takes two seconds out of your day to send something so sweet and meaningful. If he has time to check his social media, he has time to text you too!

Since I get up early, I get off work earlier. I typically wait for my BF to get home to shower. We usually catch up with one other about our day while we are showering. Don't like showering? Run a hot bubble bath, light up some candles for both of you to relax together. You are also saving water for the environment. It's a win-win!

To end the night, we love to open up a bottle of wine and binge-watch a TV show. There is nothing better than cuddling with a glass of wine and a TV show that you both enjoy! We watch The Bachelor. Yes, he loves The Bachelor- I am lucky, I know! Sometimes we bust out some lotion and give each other a foot or back rub while we watch TV. Now, ladies, you have to remember not only you had a long day, but so did he. Giving your partner a back massage is a selfless act that will satisfy your partner and who knows where the massage can lead you to. (If you know what I mean)

Do you want to score those extra brownie points with your partner? Try these everyday little romantic gestures to spice things up!

Why You Should Travel With Your BF before Saying "I DO"

You want to say it eagerly, but girl, wait!

"Living together is one thing, but traveling with your lover is a whole new ball game. Taking a trip with your boyfriend is a major step, a kind of make it or break it test for your relationship."

I wanted to put together 14 reasons why you should travel with your BF before saying, "I DO!"

12 reasons because it only took JB 14 years to finally make a move on me! Anyways, before walking down the aisle ladies, let's take a week-long trip with your lover. I suggest going somewhere out of the country. Going somewhere different with one another can help you overcome any NEW things that may disclose themselves in the future. BUT, that's just one perk! Do you really want to know if he is the one? Start here!

1. Stress: It isn't always lovey-dovey. You can come across some pretty stressful moments. Such as your plane got delayed, loss of luggage, getting bit by a million mosquitos, or figuring out where the correct direction is. This is a test to see how your man handles stress.

2. Compromise: I am sure you both want to do something new and exciting on your travel. Most times, JB & I have to compromise with one

another on where to eat, what to do, and what time we should wake up, etc. Agreeing with one another is important in a relationship. I mean, you both have to agree to say, "I do," right? So start practicing now.

3. Money: Money is always one of the top five reasons that lead to a divorce. Find out his spending habits. Talk about a budget before you travel to a new destination. This will allow you to see how responsible he is with his money.

4. Making Memories Together: How does your Mr. Right make memories with you? Does he LOVE taking pictures? Does he hate taking pictures and creating memories? If you are a picture queen (like me), you definitely need a man who will take selfies with you anytime, anywhere!

5. Interactions: You will get to see how your man interacts with strangers. I once dated a guy who was completely rude to strangers. Even the stewardess on the planes! Rude right?

6. Adapt to New Cultures: How does he adapt to change & new things? If something major happens in your life, which requires adaptation, how well are you set out to do?

7. Patience: This is something I need to do better. I am the most impatient person. BUT, thank goodness for JB always having my back. Patience is really a virtue. Let's talk kids; I don't have any, but I do have a dog. That counts, right? My mom always says you need to be patient

with your husband while raising kids. Momma is always right- you're welcome!

8. New Experiences: Does Mr. Handsome want to try new things? There is nothing sexier than a spontaneous man! You definitely don't want to marry a boring old fart.

9: Sexpectations: I think you know what I mean. Is he romantic? Having sexual attraction towards each other makes most relationships last FOREVER. So make it spicy! Make this trip feel like a honeymoon.

10. Figuring out your differences: You will be with each other 24-7. You might even get annoyed with one another. You will learn a lot about each other likes and dislikes. What your differences really are.

11. Be Present: Does he enjoy the present moment & your time together alone? Let's put the phones away for a while.

12. Comfort Zone: Sometimes, hotels in another country are a little funky. We once stayed at a place where the bathroom had no door and was open facing the bed area. How awkward would that be for your first trip together? I was once in a relationship where I felt quite uncomfortable about my body. If you are going to spend the rest of your life with someone, you better be comfortable with each other.

The ONE you should marry shouldn't just be your best friend but also your favorite travel companion. Someone who you can be comfortable with and agree to disagree. So go pack your bags and find

out if he is "The One."

How to Make Living with Your Significant Other Sexy AF

Sweet, sexy and wholesome

Living with your significant other may seem like a dream until you realize it can get awkward. Here's how to keep it sexy AF no matter what happens.

JB and I moved in quickly after about 8 months of dating. We were sleeping at each other's places almost every night, and it only made sense to take the next big step in our relationship. We both decided that it was time to take that next step everyone talks about: living together.

After some time, we quickly realized that moving in together changed our relationship a bit. While living together, most couples get too comfortable around each other, and all the sexiness is thrown out the window – I can definitely relate. Here are some tips to keep the flame burning all night long.

1. Be Playful; boys like it!

Ladies, you definitely don't want to be considered as a boring GF. Living together can get monotonous after a while, and you have to find new ways to have fun. Be playful with your lover! One of my favorite things to do is plan nerf gun wars around the house. Make it interesting by creating rules like, "whoever loses has to do whatever the other wants...in bed." This will make a living with your significant other much more exciting and sexy. The idea is simple; unpredictability!

2. Cook Together

Doing things together establishes teamwork, which you need to do anyways as a couple. Two of my favorite things to do together is showering and cooking. I mean, you are saving the environment, your water bill, and you also have someone to scrub that part of your back that you cannot. Put some music on, throw on a cute apron (only an apron) and get cooking. Someone once told me that my sandwich was "made with love." Now you can make dinner together "with love" by making love in the kitchen!

3. Marathon Sex Weeks

This was when our spark occurred. Living with your significant other can ruin the spark you used to have in the past, from not seeing each other very often. You'll end up not being in "the mood." Well, guess what? You'll need to have sex anyways. One way to get that libido back up where it used to be when you first started dating is to have a marathon sex week. This is done one week out of each month, and you have sex every single day! Yes, every day! Not only does it build excitement during the other weeks of the month, but you'll get in the mood for sex much easier.

It has been about seven months since we are officially living together, and we both look forward to coming home every day. All in all, if you're living with your significant other, you have to be sure to keep things exciting, fresh, and as sexy as possible. This is important for the longevity of your relationship.

Why you should still wear lingerie when you are married

You're missing all the fun

What the point of an outfit when it's about to get ripped off? Well babe, do you like unwrapping really pretty gifts or eating off of fine china and silver? I thoughts so! Sex is way more than just a man penetrating a woman. Yes, it's an expression of LOVE blah blah blah... BUT foreplay is more important than people give it credit for. So let's give credit where credit is due.

At first, I thought, lingerie is pointless before getting into the lingerie club. I wear it for three minutes tops, and that sixty dollar outfit is on the floor. I am also very flat-chested, so feeling sexy in lingerie was just not me. When I was dating my now-husband, I wanted to play with lingerie a lot more. It boosted my self-esteem, and he loved coming home to me. I even through wigs into the mix. It's highly important to keep those fun times alive during your marriage.

No matter where your relationship is, lingerie will help spice up any relationship! Especially for him. It keeps the imagination going and excited. Let's face it- it's in the man's DNA; love of a good fantasy. Even if it's only for those three minutes, it's FUN!

So you ask, why am I going to wear lingerie for my husband of 5 years, we already know each other's body and love each other for who we are. Let's put it this way, lingerie is like an appetizer. Get him to drool for the whole meal! It will make sex more passionate than ever. He will appreciate the extra effort and most likely perform better! YUM!

Make it more fun by making him pick out some lingerie for you! Or have a designated day for foreplay. We have been doing lingerie Sunday and let me tell you something, he loves coming home on Sundays. Sometimes he's early.

Sex

Improve your sex life

It's good for your health, duh.

So you want to improve your sex life. Most people do. Being sexual is actually one of the healthiest things a couple can do. Not only is a physical connection with someone good for your emotional health, but it is also wonderful for you physically, not to mention the pleasure. People who have active continuing sexual relationships tend to be happier and in better physical health. They also tend to live longer than counterparts who do not. When couples have happy, healthy sex lives, defined by having relations at the bare minimum of twice per month, they report being happier and dealing with the ongoing stresses of life better.

Let's discuss this.

Be truthful.

I mean two things here. Firstly, I mean to tell your partner the truth about whatever it is you feel about your sex life and how he does. If you want more frequency, ask him for it. If you want more foreplay, tell him about it. The second meaning is to be truthful about your experience: If you have trouble getting an orgasm because you need more foreplay, be

112

honest about it. If you need more kissing before penetration, say so. Truthfulness, in this context, means being honest about what you need sexually and having a clear, honest discussion with your partner. You might feel shy talking about it, but remember, the best sex comes after couples communicate about it.

Ask for whatever it is you want.

This could sound something like:

"I really need you to kiss me more and touch me outside the bedroom before we start touching each other in the bedroom."

"I want us to experiment in bed with different positions, rather than the same position as always."

"I wanted to tell you that I would like to have more foreplay when we are getting sexual before we have intercourse."

Really asking for what you want is a huge step towards having a better and more fulfilling sexual relationship. Remember, couples that have great sex do so because they have talked about it. Great sex ends up happening when you ask for what you want because it's a more fulfilling experience.

Let go.

Letting go of any possible inhibitions is a great way to make the sex better. This could mean trying to relax as much as possible during intimacy. It could mean letting go of any ideas about the way sex is supposed to look like. It could be trying a new kind of foreplay you haven't experimented with or haven't done in a long time. Letting go could also mean that you experiment with having sex with a different script, such as kissing, then intercourse, and then foreplay. Maybe letting go is trying a new position or discovering how your partner self-pleasures—which can also be a great way to find out how they like to be touched. Letting your inhibitions go with your partner can be a wonderful way to connect, build intimacy, and strengthen your relationship.

Visit a therapist/doctor.

Sometimes, medical issues can wreak havoc in a couple's sexuality. Certain prescription drugs, such as anti-depressants, sleep medications, heart medications, or allergy medications, can cause some real sexual functioning problems, including difficulties with erections, trouble having an orgasm, and lack of sexual appetite. It is good to talk to your doctor about whether any of your medications may have such side effects. Sometimes switching to a different drug can smooth things out; taking your medications opposite of when you have sex also might help. In other cases, seeing a couple's therapist together can be useful to help you talk through how you feel about your sexual relationship and to craft a plan for fixing things moving forward. Certified sex therapists can be fabulous in helping you gain solutions to sexual functioning problems, including how to last longer in bed.

Prioritize your sex life.

Things that have priority in your life are the most likely to be accomplished. If you set a goal to eat better, you are likely to be more aware of your food. If you set a goal to get more sleep, you'll go to bed earlier. If you set a goal to have a better physical relationship, you will invest more time in it. Most couples I work within my private practice decide to set a goal of trying to go to bed together at least one night a week. By going to bed together, they then increase the amount of touching, talking, kissing, and sex in the relationship overall. Not ready to go to bed together? Then talk to your partner about why not. If issues loom in the relationship, then either fix them or make peace with what they are. Disconnecting physically is bad for your relationship and for your health. By making your relationship and sex a priority, you really are investing in yourself.

Try some "dirty talk."

This is my favorite! The sexiest organ of our body is the brain; that is where sexual desire originates. This is why "dirty talk" or talking about sex in a coarse or obscene way is so arousing. Attraction starts in a part of the brain called the hypothalamus, which is responsible for the production of testosterone. The amygdala controls fear. Your reaction to dirty words or the very subject of the talk depends on these two regions of the brain, but it's different in men and women. Why do men like dirty talk? A man's hypothalamus is bigger, and therefore, they're more sexually active, and their libido is higher. The amygdala, which allows one to loosen up and reveal secret desires, is activated in the partner and makes them inclined to submission.

Get risky

Researchers assert that participation with a partner in high adrenaline activities (watching a thriller, riding a roller coaster, climbing, etc.) produces hormones that cause arousal. During stressful situations, adrenaline is released into the blood. Thereafter, the brain produces dopamine — a pleasure hormone that rewards the body for overcoming stress. After sexual activity, the affection given to your partner will certainly intensify. If you are not a thrill-seeker, exercise with your partner. The effect will be similar.

Talk afterward

Talking to your partner after sex can improve your relationship. Discussing your fantasies or things you enjoy can benefit your relationship and love life. If you can engage in frank personal pillow talk for couples, you will see positive effects.

Never Go To Bed Angry With Your Lover

Life is too short to stay angry

Going to bed angry after an argument does not solve anything. It's nothing but the easy way out; words left unsaid. I live by this rule, and to keep a healthy relationship, you and your lover should too!

The first time I moved out of my parent's house and with my ex, my mom's biggest advice was to "never go to bed angry." I never truly understood this and didn't take it too seriously until I learned firsthand.

The easy way out of an argument is to go to bed with anger instead of resolving the issue together. If you go to bed without taking care of the problem, it could easily escalate into something bigger and put your relationship at risk!

I have been in situations where my pride and stubbornness got the best of me. "Why can't my boyfriend apologize first, it's not my fault...." Anyone else does the same?

So you fall asleep, wake up the next day, and all of a sudden, there is this invisible wall built between you two, causing distance. Not only is it awkward, but you're also wasting a beautiful day being angry at each other. At some point, someone is going to have to break the wall down. Who will it be?

While we're snoozing, our brains work on organizing our experiences and placing them into our short and long-term memory, regardless of them being negative or positive. Who wants to remember an argument and all the negative things in your relationship?

A study from the University of Michigan stated, "If you will hold on to the negative emotions longer than if you had stayed awake after the contention. Sleeping will only amplify the division felt between the two."

My biggest concern when arguing with someone is guilt. Life is way too short to spend time with the attribute of anger, especially with the ones you love. What if something happens at night and your last memory of that person is that stupid little argument you had?

My now-husband, JB, hates it when I wait until we fall asleep to talk about our feelings. However, confirmation has been essential in our relationship, and we never go to bed angry. We make sure we kiss each other, no matter how tired we are, EVERY night and morning. We make sure to always say I love you even if it's annoying a million times a day.

Save yourself the awkwardness, and do not dwell in your own ego. Take the extra time to figure your issues out with your partner. Relationships are hard work, and you both should put work into it if you want it to last. It's all worth it in the long run. Trust me!

The Art of Flirting

It could be real tricky to learn how to flirt with a man. This is true if you're a little nervous and feel awkward about flirting with someone. Moreover, if you're too shy, it's much easier said than done.

Flirting has plenty of benefits and is quite fun. After a hard day at work, you really need to unwind. Go out somewhere nice with your friends and have a happy hour together. You will feel a lot better after having some drinks in you and getting to know other men outside of your circle.

Did you know that flirting can actually boost self-esteem? If you do start flirting with other men and they've become responsive, your self-confidence will get an immediate boost. That's because it feels good to be wanted. It is worth knowing that you're interesting in the eyes of a man of your choosing.

Introduce a cutie to your friend.

If you are too scared to start a conversation alone, bring a friend with you and introduce her to your crush. This may seem weird, but many times it's easier to approach a person for someone else.

Flirt before you see them:

"You should wear that black shirt tonight — it makes your eyes look amazing" This will excite them to see you later and show off that they took your advice. It will also make your crush realize that you are thinking of them.

Something cheesy, to break the ice.

If you're thinking of some pick-up lines, the only ones that are coming to your mind are probably something super lame. "So did it hurt... when you fell from heaven?" Or "So how much does an elephant weight? Just enough to break the ice!" If you are trying to play it smooth but are coming up short, embrace the awkwardness and just be cute as much as you can. You know Jughead Jones would appreciate it.

Check out their clothing!

Let's say they are wearing a band shirt or a sports jersey, ask them about it. It will make you seem sincere as well as interested in their life and will start a nice conversation where you can learn more about each other.

Be obvious, sometimes.

Maybe you're playing Frisbee at a park, and you "accidentally" throw it towards the cutie near you. An exaggerated apology makes it known that you're flirting on purpose (and in on the joke) and could easily lead to a conversation.

Ignore your crush! But not for long.

I know it sounds counter-intuitive, but imagine running into your crush and a group of their friends at McDonald's, let's say. Say hi to these friends first and strike a conversation. Your crush will feel the tiniest bit left out until you turn to include them and make their day.

The Classic bump-and-flatter.

Run into your target at a crowded party "accidentally." You can laugh and say something like, "Oh, sorry — I become a total klutz around cute people." They'll immediately be flattered and would want to know more about you. That's when you introduce yourself and start the conversation.

Let him catch you looking at them.

Yeah I know, this seems a little scary. Usually, when someone catches you staring at them, you look away so fast that they don't realize you were drooling while watching them eat a hamburger. Next time, try this instead. Gather up all the confidence you have. Then when your crush catches you staring, maintain eye contact, smile back at them, maybe even wink. It will show her that you're confident as hell and will give them the excuse to come talk to you.

BE GIRLY!

That does not mean that you act like you're a schoolgirl by being girly means that you're making him feel like the protector, despite your independence. As we learned from evolution, men are the hunters. They always protect the people they love, particularly women. That said, if you want him drawn to you, let him take the lead for a while. He would love that. Initially play it easy, wait for him to be the first one to flirt with you. Let him take charge.

Miss. MYSTERIOUS

It's not really a surprise that men love a little mystery, and I do not mean to play games with him. Just don't make yourself available for him all the time. Always leave him wanting more. If he texts you, no need to answer back straight away. Let him wait and wonder what you are doing. If he asks you out on a Saturday, tell him you have plans already, but you are available on Sunday. Show him that your time is valuable, ladies, even if you spend most of your time watching Netflix in your sweatpants.

TEXTING GAME

Everyone is texting nowadays, so make sure to use this to your advantage. Send him a little flirty message instead of the same old "How are you?" or "How's your day going?" Yawn. You can text him something like, "you have been on my mind today." My favorite rule is, wait double the time when he texted you back. He texted you back in 5 mins, wait 10 mins to text back. This will keep him waiting for more!

SEND HIM A PIC ;)

No, not that kind of pic! If you have been texting/calling the guy for some time already, and if he compliments how you look. Send him a cute smiling selfie!

The Art of Lovemaking

Coitus, have rules, ladies. Let's talk about them.
Improve sex in a relationship.

- In a relationship, communication is everything. It's how you grow as a couple, problem-solve, and get to know one another better. If you don't like it up there, just let him know. But if it is something he really likes, you could do it once in a while. Tell him what he does that get you going. Trust me, ladies, you won't regret it!

- One of the best sex tips for an amazing roll between the sheets is to set the mood. Create a romantic atmosphere is easy. Start with a clean bedroom, light some candles, put on some mood music, and start romancing your sweetheart. But that is not required. Do it when you both want, wherever you want to do it. It helps spice things up if you mix things up. Be it the couch, the kitchen counter, or tables. I wouldn't suggest doing it publicly though (but if it's your thing, go right on) Our favorite thing to do when we set the mood is play sexual music.

- Ladies, there is a good chance that your man is an animal. You, on the other hand, are definitely an animal. He has fantasies, so do you. Communicate with each other about your deepest, darkest fantasies. There will be a lot of talk about buttholes, toys and oral. So be prepared. If you can't get off, talk about toys, it can help.

- Doing a little roleplay in the bedroom is a great way to boost your sex life. Let your imagination run wild and feel the heat radiating between the sheets. You can be the naughty babysitter, seductress secretary and boss, vixen elf, and magical mage. Whatever your fantasy is, roleplay it!

- Who doesn't enjoy getting oral sex? If you are not into that stuff, there is a good chance that your partner is. He might not communicate it to you as he knows it's not your thing. Little sacrifices in a relationship can go a long way.

- Speaking of Oral sex, it is a two-way street. While it could feel awesome, you need to give it back. Don't be selfish in the bed, then be crying when they cheat! Suck him dry and fill his belly, and he shall never leave.

- Foreplay is important. Really important. Not only is kissing, touching, caressing, and pleasuring your partner a good way to connect before getting down to the deed, but it's also a great way to ensure a better orgasm. Slow things down by taking control and setting up the pace yourself by being the aggressor if you feel like the sex doesn't last long. This is something I had to bring back up to the hubby. You two might be so comfortable you just go straight to having sex. However, play with each other more beforehand. It gets you more in the mood and makes intimacy last longer!

- Remember when you first moved in together and were able to express yourself as loud as you wanted to during sex? Well, get the kids a babysitter tonight, because it's time to get verbal.

- Don't be afraid of a little dirty talk every now and then. Roleplaying or getting a little crude is a great way to turn each other one and live out a fantasy. It's more important for men, as women get turned on by words more than men.

- Great sex doesn't come with a timer. If you really want to have better sex, make sure you have a good amount of time set aside for it. Many people try to force themselves to orgasm or rush to have an orgasm, which could be more satisfying if they slowly built towards it. While there is nothing wrong with a quick encounter, try building to a slow burn and know that you don't both have to come at the same time, as long as you both enjoy what you are doing and stay connected. Pace yourselves and build slowly towards the orgasms, playing it off each other. It's good to build excitement, slow down, and build it back up. Lower and raise the intensity until you choose to let it go and have an orgasm.

- One of the best sex tips for hotter lovemaking is to focus on your emotional connection. Spend quality time together, bonding outside of the bedroom, and you'll see your sex life, as well as your relationship, improve.

- Research (disturbingly) shows that 1 in 10 couples admit to checking their phones WHILE HAVING SEX! Crazy right? Being intimate with your partner and working on your orgasm is the last occasion on earth, you should be catching up on your texts. Do yourselves both a favor by turning your phones to silent and putting them in a drawer for the duration of the ride.

- Studies show that physical affection, such as holding hands, kissing, cuddling, and massaging one another, is strongly related to relationship satisfaction. Sex is never all about fire in the hole. There is a big difference in having sex and making love. A strong connection makes all the difference!

- Understand. He comes back from work and is tired. He might not be in the mood for sex. Nothing's wrong with that, and instead of whining, try to seduce him and do most of the work. Appreciate your man. BUT also make sure he appreciates you back, ladies.

- Speaking about appreciation. Always appreciate your partner's sexual ability. It not only boosts his confidence, but he will also try to do an even better job the next time.

- We all have insecurities. We feel insecure when someone passes comment on something we are not really proud of. Your partners is not another person, he is you, or a part of you, at least. Never make fun of his insecurities, which is hard because when you're a woman, and he does something wrong, all that he has done wrong in his life comes pouring out of us with the attention of ultimate destruction. This can have a huge effect on what goes on in the bedroom. Control your anger, when you start seeing red, stop. Don't cut so deep to the point of no return.

- Being "Sexy" is a state of mind, regardless of your age or size. Much often, we can turn ourselves off long before our partner even enters the bedroom. Embrace your sexiness. Your energy does indeed affect your partner. Find the tools in your personal toolbox to turn yourself on, whether it's what you wear, the smile on your face, or even the relaxation you feel when you light your favorite candle. We all have a responsibility and opportunity to embrace our inner sexy. Do it, and I promise you will reap great rewards in the bedroom.

- Eye contact. I'm not talking about a glance, I mean a true gaze. Gazing into your partner's eyes can actually raise arousal and foster intimacy. For many couples, this could be an extremely awkward task. Because the gaze is quite intimate, many couples avoid this powerful aphrodisiac. They feel vulnerable. However, this exercise can be a powerful and therapeutic intervention for couples who want to reconnect or even take their connection to an even deeper level.

- Mix it up. We spoke about spicing it up, but intercourse in the same old position can be boring. Keep it exciting by trying new stuff. Watch porn together, if that's your thing. But remember to be innovative. Remember, sex is an art, with practice you can get better at it.

"Sex is an art, and not everyone is an artist" - **Sristichara**

CPSIA information can be obtained
at www.ICGtesting.com
Printed in the USA
BVHW040218031221
623153BV00015B/1120